But What If I Fail

But What If I Fail

George D. Martin Jr.

iUniverse, Inc.
New York   Bloomington

iUniverse books may be ordered through booksellers or by contacting:

iUniverse
1663 Liberty Drive
Bloomington, IN 47403
www.iuniverse.com
1-800-Authors (1-800-288-4677)

Because of the dynamic nature of the Internet, any Web addresses or
links contained in this book may have changed since publication and
may no longer be valid. The views expressed in this work are solely those
of the author and do not necessarily reflect the views of the publisher,
and the publisher hereby disclaims any responsibility for them.

ISBN: 978-1-4401-4759-3 (sc)
ISBN: 978-1-4401-4760-9 (ebook)

Printed in the United States of America

iUniverse rev. date: 06/17/2009

Contents

Introduction

The fear of failure is one of the most gripping and paralyzing of all fears. True fulfillment in life is many times severely limited simply by the fear of failure. This fear often manifests itself in the lack of taking risks or trying new experiences or perhaps listening to God's calling in our lives. We often find reasons (that are actually disguised excuses) as to why the "time is not right," or we're waiting for "things to come together better," or we'll take advantage of "the next opportunity." Unfortunately, the final result is no action. In like manner, there are many of us who love God and desire to please Him with our lives, but we sit on the spiritual sidelines watching. We choose not to participate not because we have nothing to contribute, or have not been sent into the game. Rather, through our non-response, we have chosen, or even demanded, to remain on the sidelines. Many times we have concluded, not because we truly believe it but because of fear of failure, that the cause is better served with our remaining where we are.

I can remember a young man from my high school basketball team that never missed a practice, was always on time for practices, and even gave his best effort throughout the practices. However, when it came to actually playing in the game, he became nervous and afraid. I recall one specific time in an intense game when we were short manned because of foul trouble, the coach called for him to go into the game. The coach called his name and he just sat there. The coach again called him, but still no response. He sat there as though he wasn't being called. Finally the coach called another player and sent him into the game. Afterwards, I recall overhearing the coach saying to him, "Son, if you are not here to play, then why are you here?" It seems that he was afraid of going into the game, making a mistake, and then having to wrestle with the feeling of having failed.

Those of us who are a part of the family of God, like the young man from my high school basketball team, have been called on to play a role. We have been charged by a great commissioning that compels us and challenges us to labor to build the kingdom of God on earth. *"Go therefore and make disciples of all nations, baptizing them in the name of the Father and of the Son and of the Holy Spirit, teaching them to observe all things that I have commanded you; and lo, I am with you always, even to the end of the age."* (Matthew 28:19-20) We comprise what would be considered the "Kingdom Team." We have been recruited by Jesus Christ to advance the Kingdom of God on earth. This team has a Champion leader, whose great victories inspire us as they challenge us to live our lives for Him, and accomplish great things through Him. As with any great team, each one of us has been called on to play a specific role on the team. We all have unique abilities, experiences, gifts and talents that when brought together create something amazingly exciting and powerful. However, in far too many cases, we have been called on yet we have remained seated, as though we have not been called on at all, because we sit almost paralyzed asking *"But what if I fail?"*

This book is inspired by the story of God's calling of one of the most familiar of all biblical personalities - Moses, as it is recorded in Exodus 3:1- 4:17. Moses, the most admired and most recognized of all Hebrew leaders, didn't have the greatest start as a leader. Actually, his start was one of uncertainty and doubt. He lacked confidence in himself and his abilities. He was reluctant and afraid. He felt that his inabilities overshadowed his abilities. He was more focused on the things that he felt would hinder him from leading as opposed to the things that would help him to lead; most importantly, God's calling of him and expressed desire to use him, which essentially was establishing Moses' leadership capability.

I am convinced that to some degree there is a bit of this attitude in all of us; an attitude that struggles to see good qualities, but overindulges in spotlighting the lesser qualities. If you ask many of us to list ten things we really like about ourselves with a limited amount of time to respond, say 30 seconds, we would probably need some additional time to think of ten things. We might even, in some cases, struggle to complete the list. On the other hand, if you ask us to list ten things we dislike about ourselves, having only the same 30 seconds, we would likely complete the list before the expiration of the allotted time to respond. In fact, the list might exceed the number of items requested. Most of us will agree that we are our own harshest critics. However, criticism when used constructively, as in helping to further develop possibilities, can be of great benefit. Conversely, criticism when used to only highlight failures or areas where we lack ability can play the role of our enemy or adversary. Personally, I can say, I am one who critiques practically everything I say and do. This in many cases results in my focusing more on what is wrong or flawed rather than on the things that are of good quality or which are an asset to me.

This type of mindset, of overemphasizing lacks or failure, or even the possibility of failure, can be a tremendous hindrance when it comes to God's desire to use us for His kingdom. His calling of us to action becomes subject to our mind and our thoughts, and not according to His mind and His will. We are encouraged through God's word to know that God doesn't think of us in the ways that we sometimes think of ourselves. *"For My thoughts are not your thoughts, Nor are your ways My way says the Lord."* (Isaiah 55:8) *"For I know that thoughts that I think toward you, says the Lord, thoughts of peace and not of evil, to give you a future and a hope."* (Jeremiah 29:11) There is an assurance that can be gained in knowing that the thoughts and plans God has for our lives are for our good and for His glory. However, if we forfeit this assurance by being predisposed to what we think will prevent us from being used by God, we find that more often than not we respond as Moses did. That is, we do not respond favorably to the calling because we are responding according to the perception *we* have of ourselves as opposed to trusting *God's* knowledge of us. Our God knows the beginning and end of all things, and knows the hidden abilities and gifts that have been deposited in each of us, that will never be discovered unless they are activated and uncovered as we walk in daily trust of God and His abilities at work through us. We must remember that God does not always call upon those who are equipped, but He always equips those He calls.

Before we go further, I would like to highlight some passages from Moses' exchange with God that will establish a clear understanding of Moses' state of being at the time of God's calling of him. This will help us develop the premise from which to draw as we further gain insights.

"But Moses said to God, Who am I that I should go to Pharaoh, and that I should bring the children of Israel out of Egypt?" (**Exodus 3:11**)

"Then Moses answered and said, But suppose they will not believe me or listen to my voice; suppose they say, The Lord has not appeared to you." (**Exodus 4:1**)

"Then Moses said to the Lord, O my Lord I am not eloquent, neither before nor since You have spoken to Your servant; but I am slow of speech and slow of tongue." (**Exodus 4:10**)

"But he said, O my Lord, please send by the hand of whomever else You may send." (**Exodus 4:13**)

It is important here for me to stress that highlighting these responses of Moses are not to suggest a cowardly nature on the part of Moses, for it should be understood that the assignment God was assigning to him was great! He was one man, being sent to the Pharaoh (leader) of a great nation, without an army or military allies, and demand of the Pharaoh to release the slaves that had brought him and his nation great wealth and prosperity. An assignment of this magnitude could provoke fear in even the bravest of men. These verses are only intended to bring definition to a state of mind that can be shared by any *born-again* believer in Christ when feeling compelled by God to do something they have never done, or something that seems too far out of their capacity to do.

Now I do realize that not all of us are called to leadership, but we *are* all called to some part or role in God's kingdom. Certainly we are not all called in the traditional sense, as one feels called into full-time ministry, or called to be a missionary or traveling evangelist. However, we *are* all called to affect our individual areas of influence and take advantage of opportunities to be used by God in even the smallest ways. We can agree and accept that not everyone is called or expected to be a Moses, a leader who has impacted millions of lives. However, that does not excuse us for not impacting the lives that we each individually have been charged by God to affect.

As you read this book, my hope is that a seed of a different way of thinking, when it comes to God desiring to use us, will be planted. And that this seed will result in, or develop into, greater insight as to what you are capable of accomplishing when it is God who is giving the assignment and equipping you to fulfill the purpose.

Chapter One
Inability vs. Ability

In looking at Moses as our example, and drawing our observations from the scene of his commissioning by God to go into Egypt and free the Children of Israel from their slavery, we see that he was familiar with tending sheep due to his extended tenure working as a shepherd for his father-in-law, Jethro. In his capacity as a shepherd, we can assume, he believed he functioned well and that caring for Jethro's sheep had become so familiar to him that it now seemed to be second nature. His shepherding abilities created for him a good sense of himself and his abilities, and allowed him to feel self-confidence and self-assured in his ability to perform the work assigned to him. However, tending the sheep also allowed him to hide or avoid situations in which he didn't feel secure, or did not have a good sense of aptitude in. For instance, his speech impediment didn't matter with the sheep because they didn't care what he sounded like, or how fluent or eloquent he was. ***"O my Lord, I am not eloquent, neither before nor since You have spoken to Your servant; but I am slow of speech and slow of tongue."*** (Exodus 4:10) As a matter of fact, he didn't have to say very much to them at all. He could simply issue a few minor commands and then help to guide the sheep with the staff in his hand. Therefore, he could feel confident that he was a good shepherd and was doing a good job without his inabilities interfering. With the sheep, Moses wasn't concerned about what they thought of him or if they believed enough in him to follow him. ***"But suppose they will not believe me or listen to my voice; suppose they say, 'The Lord has not appeared to you.'"*** (Exodus 4:1) The sheep followed his leading without questioning who he was or where he got his direction. So you see, when God came to Moses asking him to be His vessel of deliverance to an estimated two million enslaved Hebrew men, women and children in Egypt, Moses was very concerned about his transition from the sheep to God's people, and how well he would fare in this new environment.

Under the circumstance, Moses needed only to realize that God, when calling him, had already established his ability. God, who has all ability, was going to supply Moses with the ability and bring forth out of him the things that to this point were still hidden in him. Therefore, Moses' inability to speak well, his lack of confidence in standing before the king, or his fear of leading the people were all subject to the purpose God had for him. God knew that the hidden things within Moses were about to be brought forth as he walked in obedience. Moses, by submitting to the will and calling of God, even though reluctant, placed himself in a position of destiny. Moses was now in the hands of the great *Potter* who was going to change him from a vessel of dishonor to a vessel of great honor.

You see, Moses was already leading, yet he did not see that he already possessed some key ingredients for good leadership. He

2

possessed the care, concern, and watchfulness of a good leader. These qualities were some of the things that would make Moses the right man for the job of leading God's people out of Egypt. Let me explain. As a competent shepherd, Moses had led the sheep to feed in areas where the food was good for their digestion. He had chosen feeding places where the food was plentiful enough so that all could eat. He had watched the surrounding area and kept the sheep safe from harmful predators. He also had to be aware of their positioning to guard against the sheep wandering too far or into danger. These were all things that had become second nature to him. However, because these leadership abilities had become second nature to Moses, he failed to fully appreciate the significance of them. So often, when assessing our abilities, things that are familiar to us or that are natural for us, go unnoticed. This is all part of a battle that is waged persistently within our minds which we will call the battle of *Inability vs. Ability*.

The leadership abilities that God had been developing in Moses while he was hiding in self-security were hidden to him. And without his obedience to God's calling of him, he may never have discovered them. Because of Moses' self-doubt, God gives him Aaron, his brother, to assist him; and we see that initially Aaron is speaking on behalf of Moses. However, we later find that Moses begins speaking for himself, as he continues to walk in obedience to God's calling and his hidden abilities begin to emerge. There are things within us that have been placed there by God which will never be discovered until we submit to God's calling of us. Oftentimes without our knowing, God has planted and has been

3

cultivating things within us that He has purposed to use in the building and establishment of His earthly Kingdom. Fortunately, in Moses' case, he ultimately accepted God's commission to do the things that he himself felt should be the last thing God should be asking him to do. The Bible tells us that God's ways are not our ways, and His thoughts are not our thoughts. (Isaiah 55:8) Therefore, the things that God calls us to do may seem so discordant with what we believe our strengths and abilities to be that, in many cases, we reject God's request because we do not see ourselves the way He sees us. God sees us based upon the things that He has deposited within us, or the agenda He has established for us to complete. These are hidden qualities and abilities which in many cases we are not aware exist.

The Battle in the Mind

There is a battle that wages in our mind, the battle of *Inability vs. Ability*, which is often dominated by our thoughts of inability or feelings of inadequacy. When our thoughts are dominated by our inabilities, the recall of the things we do well can become suppressed and create a state of inactivity or a returning to things we feel most comfortable doing. As a result, we remain ensnared in limited places of functionality where we are most comfortable. More often than we may realize or admit, fear creates our sense of inability which in turn fosters inactivity and non-response. In some cases, our agonizing over whether or not we should move forward by faith and simply yield to God's leading of us results in unfulfilled purposes God has intended in our lives. Due to fear, we fail to engage a new challenge or opportunity to which He has called us. The Bible exclaims that *"fear involves torment"* or that fear can torment (I John 4:18), and we understand that torment includes restraint; this restraint can keep us from experiencing the liberation of walking in faith and obedience when God wills to use us.

Fear has the ability to paralyze and perpetuate a feeling of inability. Many non-decisions are the result of fear and its' paralyzing effects. For this reason, the Apostle Paul declares in his letter to the young church leader, Timothy, (when trying to encourage him to not be afraid to follow God's calling): *"For God has not given us a spirit of fear, but of power and of love and of a sound mind."* (2 Timothy 1:7) Paul was trying to remind Timothy that God had empowered him, and therefore whatever he lacked or whatever inability he possessed was subject to the empowerment of God. God would enable and empower Timothy to carry out His will. Therefore, he should stand in a position of power, actively pursuing the fulfillment of his calling, and not be handicapped by his disabling feelings of inadequacy.

It is true of many of us, that if we asked ourselves the question "what am I good at," depending on the time in our lives the question is asked, we will have varied responses. As a teenager, our answer may center on relationships with friends, school activities or athletics. As a young adult, our answer may center on our academic studies, professional plans or personal expression. As an adult, our answer may center on hobbies, parenting, marriage or professional accomplishments. The response will essentially be based upon the things we consider ourselves to be good at doing. This all hinges upon what we have done, and feel we have fared well in. This becomes our "place of familiarity" and comfort, which most often becomes the well from which we draw to define our abilities. We tend to confine ourselves to the familiar and things we feel we are "good at." We generally find that we define our abilities based primarily on what is familiar to us, and our inability on what is not as familiar to us. What we've always done seems to make so much more sense to do than the things we have not done that are unfamiliar to us. These habits are consistent with an age-old human factor called "fear of the unknown." As human beings, we are creatures of habit or creatures of the "familiar." However, God specializes in bringing we humans, the masters of the familiar, into close acquaintance with the unfamiliar.

For the sake of our discussion, let us consider the Gospel message here. God perfectly orchestrated His master plan in taking mankind, who is born sinful in nature and is most familiar with sin, and brought us into close acquaintance with righteousness, with which we were not familiar, through Jesus Christ. Without Christ we were experts of sin and had terribly failed when it came to being righteous. However, where our ability lacked, Christ made up the difference.

"For all have sinned and fall short of the glory of God."

(Romans 3:23)

"For when we were still without strength, in due time Christ died for the ungodly."

(Romans 5:6)

"And therefore it was accounted to him for righteousness. Now it was

not written for his sake alone that it was imputed to him, but also for us. It shall be imputed to us who believe in Him who raised up Jesus our Lord from the dead, who was delivered up because of our offenses, and was raised because of our justification."

(Romans 4:22-25)

"For He made Him who knew no sin to be sin for us, that we might become the righteousness of God in Him."

(II Corinthians 5:21)

With this understanding, God knows how to compensate for our lack, thus we can gain assurance to know that He is able again to make up the difference in us when He uses us.

You're Sure You Want Me?

I must admit personally when I felt God was calling me into the ministry and ultimately to Pastoring, I could not envision myself serving Him in either of these capacities. By nature I am a shy person who prefers to exist without drawing much attention to myself. The idea of standing before large groups of people to speak was very intimidating and frightening. But like Moses, there were things that I was doing and had done in the past which had developed within me abilities that were hidden to me. Even when the time had come that I would pastor, which would require my interaction with many types of people on many different levels, I felt very uncomfortable about the idea. I think I would best be described as an "introverted extrovert," preferring to be alone with not much to say. Having come from a very large family, however, I have acquired the ability to interrelate and interact with an array of personality types and personal temperaments. In a similar way, Moses while serving as a shepherd for his father-in-law, Jethro, unknowingly was being cultivated as a leader. He was learning to care for, instruct, and direct through his shepherding responsibilities. Just as the flocks of sheep were not his, but his father-in-law, Jethro's, yet he had learned to care for them, Moses would now learn to lead the people that belonged to God and that God had entrusted to his care. As he had received his instructions from Jethro pertaining to the sheep, he would now receive his instructions from the Most-High God pertaining to His people. As he had lead the flocks of Jethro through the challenging terrain of Midian and back of the desert to Horeb, he gained experience in being able to manage and understood how to live in the desert climate. He would now draw on that experience and lead the people of God for 40 years in the desert.

As a part of God's confirming within me what He was calling me to, He reminded me of different experiences that I had had, responsibilities I had maintained, and even duties I at that time possessed, which had all required me to utilize skills necessary for me to be an effective minister of the gospel and ultimately a senior pastor. As I accepted the commission and began to walk in obedience to God's calling, I began to further realize gifts, talents, and abilities that were deposited in me by God to fulfill his purpose for my life; things that would allow me to fulfill my role on the team He has assembled to build His kingdom on earth. These were gifts and talents that God always knew I possessed, but that I could not know until I submitted to His designed plan for my life. God was making up the difference in me, and causing me to become something I could not have become without Him. Paul realized this as he writes in his epistle to the church in Philippi *"I can do all things through Christ, who strengthens me."* (Philippians 4:13) In others words, through Christ who enables or "ables" me, I can do all things.

He Can Do It

"When Jesus departed from there, two blind men followed Him, crying out and saying 'Son of David, have mercy on us!' And when He had come into the house, the blind men came to Him. And Jesus said to them, 'Do you believe that I am able to do this?' They said to Him, 'Yes, Lord.' Then He touched their eyes, saying, According to your faith let it be to you." (Matthew 9:27-29)

An observation from this story will help us further develop our point that when God is involved our aptitude changes. The two men came to Jesus and needed Him to help them do something they had never before done, and that without Him they would not be able to do. The two men wanted Him to help them to see. It is worth noting here, and even highlighting, that Jesus asks them "Do you believe I am *able* to do this?" Do you believe I am *able* to help you to do something that you have never done before? The two men emphatically responded with "Yes, Lord." It seems that in our times of fear and uncertainty, when our fear of failure has gripped and imprisoned us and would hold us hostage and keep us from stepping out in faith, God is saying to us "Do you believe I am able to help you?" In those times, if we would respond as the two blind men did, with an emphatic "Yes, Lord," we would experience, as they did, God do something in us that has not been done before. There are two very distinct adjectives which describe God that seem to have in some ways drifted off of the radar screens of many Christians; *Sovereign* and *Omnipotent*. God being *Sovereign* means that He is superior above all others, supreme in power, rank and authority, and is independent of all others. The one hundred and fifteenth division of Psalm verse three declares this of Him: *"But our God is in heaven, He does whatever He pleases."* Consequently, we can conclude that He also can use whomever He chooses, the way He chooses. God being *Omnipotent* means that He is almighty, all-powerful, and His power is infinite and unlimited. He says this about himself in Genesis 35:11: *"Also God said to him: 'I am God Almighty.'"* When we are being drawn by God, and have been assigned by Him a purpose He wants to accomplish through us, we cannot allow ourselves to forget that He is a *Sovereign* and *Omnipotent* God, who shares His abilities with us, which cancels out our inability. Therefore, because He is far beyond able, we are more than able through Him.

Chapter 2

Moses in Me

Inside of everyone there is a part of us that is convinced we are much more limited than we actually are. It is that part of us that hesitates and even cringes in the presence of an opportunity that demands us to stretch further than we have before or go where we've never gone before; more specifically, an opportunity that requires us to trust God more than we have ever trusted Him, in a way that we've never trusted Him, for something we have never trusted Him.

Feeling more limited than we actually are is the more easily identifiable characteristic of Moses to which we may be able to relate. However, I would like to help to identify the undiscovered Moses that remains barred within. The Moses that soared higher than he ever imagined. Accomplishing things he never imagined. Becoming someone he never imagined. Being used by God in a way he never imagined. Moses never saw himself leading God's people, yet he grew up as a member of the household of an Egyptian leader. There were things that were deposited in him while observing, listening and living in the Pharaoh's household that would help him to understand the role of a leader and how to

George D. Martin Jr.

later govern a large group of people, and judge matters pertaining to the daily lives of that group of people. Things inside of him that he was not aware existed, hidden abilities.

Hidden Within

> **"But Moses said to God, Who am I that I should go to Pharaoh, and that I should bring the children of Israel out of Egypt?"**
>
> **(Exodus 3:11)**

At the time of his commissioning by God, Moses' idea of who he was and what he was able to do was very limited. In this eleventh verse of Exodus chapter three he seems to dejectedly proclaim, *"Who am I that I should go to Pharaoh."* It is as if he is saying I am nobody to even go and request the audience of a Pharaoh, let alone declare anything to him or make any demands of him. I would like to emphasize that in our observation of Moses, I want to be sure that we do not fail to recognize and acknowledge that the magnitude of what he was being asked to do was very great. This calling would invoke fear and hesitation in even the bravest, most proven men, or even great leaders of nations with armies and military support systems. For Moses was being asked as one man without a great and powerful army behind him or any military allies to go to the head of a great nation and demand the release of a whole nation of people that his country had enslaved and benefited from their labor, skills and expertise for hundreds of years. This was certainly no small assignment. Yet it was something that God was assigning him to do, and even assuring him that we would be able to accomplish it.

As we further develop this idea of hidden abilities within, I would like to draw from the experiences of some other well-known Bible personalities. Although there are a number of characters in the Bible that were the products of hidden deposits within them, in this chapter we will highlight only three men of the Bible in addition to Moses who accomplished great things and became great even though it was not visibly evident; namely, King David, the Apostle Paul and Apostle Peter. These are three men whose individual stories yield three different perspectives in understanding that when God is a factor in the equation, there are hidden potentials that lie within all of us.

King David

David, before becoming king of Israel, was so unassuming that his father almost forgot to mention him when the prophet Samuel came to anoint one of his sons to become the next king. Here's how the story unfolds. God had rejected Saul, Israel's first king, because of His disobedience. And now God was choosing another king, so He sent Samuel, His servant, to anoint the man whom He had chosen. He had told Samuel that the next king would be one of the sons of Jesse the Bethlehemite. After having examined all of David's seven older brothers, Samuel asks David's father, Jesse, if he has any other sons. And as though it were an afterthought, Jesse mentions David. We should pause here to note that Jesse had eagerly presented all of his other sons. However, it is not until Samuel declares that none of the other sons would be anointed king, and inquires as to whether there are any other sons that Jesse might present, that Jesse suggests David. In spite of being overlooked or in this case under-looked,

David still became Israel's second king, and one of its greatest kings. The courage and strength to be a great king rested deep down inside of a young man described as "ruddy." Jesse, David's father, seems to forget about him while trying to present his other seven sons. Although Jesse didn't see David as a king, God had chosen him as His next king. Because so much of what we know as human beings we have observed with our eyes, it seems only human nature to place a lot of confidence in what we see. For this reason, God had to instruct Samuel while he was examining David's older brothers not to consider their visible attributes. *"Do not look at his appearance or at his physical stature, because I have refused him. For the Lord does not see as man sees; for man looks at the outward appearance, but the Lord looks at the heart."* (I Samuel 16:7) Samuel would later need to apply these same instructions when he would see small "ruddy" David. These instructions were necessary because God wanted Samuel to know that He was not selecting His new king based upon external appearance, but what was on the inside, in his heart. Like David, there are many individuals that on the outside don't look like much, but on the inside there is greatness. There may be things that God knows are within you that even your family may not realize about you or see in you, things that they may later be proud of, but that are just not easily detected in you. God recognized the courage and strength of a great king that was in David, but hidden from view. As in David's case, when God desires to use you, He recognizes the things in your heart that others have not seen, and that you may have yet to discover; abilities and opportunities to be and to do what even those who are closest to you, or those who should really know you, have not predicted of you. The awesome thing about David's story, your story, and even my own story, is that what God wanted to do through David or wants to do through you is not contingent upon others realizing it about you, or believing it about you. It depends solely on God's knowledge of us and the plans He has for our lives, and for the purposes He has assigned each of our lives.

The Apostle Paul

We will now turn our attention to another great man of the Bible, the Apostle Paul, who tirelessly committed himself to the persecution of Christians and the Christ movement of his day. What Apostle Paul did not realize, however, was that all the things he had heard from the Christians about Jesus the Christ were actually deposits of information that would allow him to become one of the greatest evangelist the church has ever known. He is also arguably the greatest author the church has ever known, contributing nearly half the books of the New Testament. In all of his endeavors, he had encountered the testimonies and witness of prisoners and martyrs that had little by little exposed him to the gospel message of Jesus Christ.

In the seventh chapter of Acts we see Saul, who later became Paul the Apostle, standing and listening while Stephen preaches a synoptic sermon just before he is stoned to death as a martyr. Stephen, beginning with Abraham, showed how all the great events of the Hebrew people were in harmony with and leading up to the coming of Christ and His fulfillment of God's plan. Young Saul stood watch over the clothes of the men as they stoned Stephen. Later, his very conversion takes place while he is on a requested assignment to persecute more Christians living in Damascus. Imagine that, a man who exhibits such vigor and determination in stopping the spread of the gospel became such a champion for the furtherance of that same gospel; a champion that the world has not since known. It's amazing how a man who was zealous and committed to things that were *against* God would now be as adamantly zealous and committed to the things he would do *for* God. The same fervor he had in his persecution of Christians, he would now demonstrate in his pursuit of convincing more souls to a hope in Christ. Far too often, we become dedicated and committed to people, clubs, groups, organizations, activities, and hobbies that do not honor God in our lives, or take precedence over God in our lives. We become willing to give all we have to those pursuits, and even some cases search for ways in which we can enhance and further develop pursuits which are not in line with God's plan for us.

Yet unlike Paul, many times our zeal and dedication do not transfer to those pursuits that honor and serve God. We are not dedicated to enhance the kingdom of God, nor to the development of the kingdom, or looking for ways in which we might help the kingdom to grow. However, like Paul, there are things that we have done before coming into a relationship with God, through Jesus Christ, that did not bring glory and honor to God; things that God may now want to use in His kingdom and for His glory. It may be something that you never would have thought you could or would do for God, but your dedication and commitment to it will allow you to flourish in it and consequently enhance God's kingdom. There may be skills, talents, or expertise that you have obtained during your time of living out of fellowship with God that can now be used in your service for Him. God knew that Saul, the persecutor of

Christians, would become Paul the Apostle of Jesus Christ, the great Evangelist, and a Crusader for Christianity, even though it originally seemed very much out of character for him and not even a possibility.

The Apostle Peter

Finally let's examine the Apostle Peter. He was one who was well acquainted with failing and mistakes. His faulty walk on the water, his misspeak in suggesting that three tabernacles should be built on the mountain where Jesus was transfigured, his cutting off the soldier's ear in the garden of Gethsemane during Jesus' arrest, and of course his well-known denial of knowing Jesus Christ three times. Yet on the day of Pentecost he stands and preaches and delivers such a powerful message that about 3,000 people are added to the church in one day. A fisherman by trade, Peter was well aware of how to gather fish. He knew the proper techniques in gathering, he knew the best times to gather, he knew the right tools to use in gathering. However, Jesus knew that his abilities were not limited to gathering fish. For when Jesus saw Peter and his brother Andrew fishing, He called to them and said *"Follow Me, and I will make you fishers of men."* (Mathew 4:19) His skill of fishing would now be used to fish for the lost souls of men. On the day of Pentecost, Peter put all of his skills to use, and his first catch was possibly his greatest catch in his new occupation of fisherman of men. Peter used his understanding of timing, for when the men began to mock he and the disciples after receiving the Holy Ghost, suggesting that he and the other disciples were drunk, he stood and spoke in such a way that he grabbed their attention. (Acts 2:14) Peter used his understanding of technique, when identifying with his audience: *"Men of Judea, and all who dwell in Jerusalem"* (Acts 2:14); *"Men of Israel"* (Acts 2:22); for He was able to gain their audience. He used his understanding of proper tools when he tied God's word, the Holy Scriptures (Acts 2:17-20, 25-28, 34-35), to God's "Word", being Jesus Christ the "Word" that became flesh and dwelt among men. (John 1:14) The Living Word!

In each case, each man had undiscovered abilities within him that he did not know existed, but God knew. In following God's calling in their lives, they were able to discover these hidden abilities in themselves and use them for the glory of God. God called them based not so much on what they had done, but more so on what they could do in Him. As with each of these men, when God is tugging at you heart and calling you to His vineyard, He does consider what you have done, but He is more concerned with what you are able to do.

Chapter Three

Is it My Calling?

God oftentimes has plans for us that don't match the known skills we regularly exercise on a daily basis. We all have various roles and parts God has desired for us to play in the Body of Christ for the building of His earthly kingdom. These roles may not match the capacities in which we are currently functioning, or they may not be roles that we have ever envisioned ourselves being able to perform. Yet God still desires to use us in fulfilling these various needs.

When we look at the account of Moses' commissioning, we see that it is God who visits Moses and says to him I have something for you to do. *"Come now, therefore, and I will send you to Pharaoh that you may bring My people, the children of Israel, out of Egypt."* (Exodus 3:10) God says that God has something for Moses to do. However, Moses, because he was not presently functioning as a leader and deliverer of men, immediately responds with reluctance and surprise. ***"Who am I that I should go to Pharaoh, and that I should bring the children of Israel, out of Egypt."*** (Exodus 3:11) The Creator of heaven and earth and everything on the earth, the very God who knows all things, and knows things about each

19

of us we don't know about ourselves, or may not realize about ourselves, was calling him to do something that he had never done nor had even dreamed of doing. What Moses didn't realize was that it was God's "calling," and because the calling originated from God, it was God's responsibility to choose the right person and enable that person to accomplish what He was calling him to do. Without over emphasis, I would like to once again point out that it is <u>God's calling of him</u>. In calling him, God knew the part of Moses that Moses himself had not discovered and did not realize existed. God had predetermined that He had some work He wanted to complete, and Moses was the vessel He would use to complete it. *"Come now, therefore, and I will send you to Pharaoh that you may bring My people, the children of Israel, out of Egypt."* (Exodus 3:10) What had not become clear to Moses at this point was that God knew all about Moses when He charged him to go and complete the assignment He was giving him. God was aware of his lack of confidence, so God assured him that He would be with him. *"I will certainly be with you."* (Exodus 3:12) God was aware of his speaking impediment. Therefore, God told Moses to simply open his mouth and He would speak for him. *"Who has made man's mouth? Or who has made the mute, the deaf, the seeing, or the blind? Have not I, the Lord? Now therefore go, and I will be with your mouth and teach you what you shall say."* (Exodus 4:11-12) In spite of Moses' limitations and challenges, God was still enlisting his service because God knew that Moses was the right person for the job. God was going to make the difference, in that He was going to equip, or had already equipped, Moses with the necessary aptitudes to complete the assignment which He requested of him.

Many of us make the same mistake when God has assigned something to our hands. We are able at times to state with confidence "God knows all things," but somehow a disconnect happens when it comes to God's calling of us into the purpose He has assigned to us to fulfill. We lose sight of the fact that if God does truly know all things, He must know about all of the insecurity, shortcomings and failures through which we function each day. By making this disconnect, we have so often limited God and have essentially tied God's hands. God chooses to use us, but we must also choose to accept His choosing. If we take a close look at Ephesians 3:20, honing in on the latter part of the verse, we can see that God is able to do exceedingly and abundantly above all that we ask or think, but that ability is *"according to the power that works in us."*

The Master Builder

And what is the power at work in us, you may ask. Well, it is our <u>faith</u> according to I John 5:4 *"...and this is the victory* (or that which empowers us to be victorious) *that has overcome the world, our <u>faith</u>."* The kind of faith in our God that believes He is able to do the extraordinary. Faith to believe that God really does know all things and therefore knows that in entrusting something to us to complete, He is already aware of the things that may be obstacles for us, but more so He is aware of our ability through Him to complete it. Any good Master Builder chooses the right resources to get the job done. And not just get the job done, but get the job done right. God, the *"Great Master Builder,"* when choosing, chooses carefully. *"The Stone which the builders rejected Has become the chief cornerstone. This was the Lord's doing; It is marvelous in our eyes."* (Psalm 118:22-23) *"Behold, I lay in Zion* *a stone for a foundation, A tried stone, a precious cornerstone, a sure foundation."* (Isaiah 28:16) Being careful to select the right tools, God chooses the right materials to ensure the job is performed well and is performed right. Just as He chose Jesus to be the Chief Cornerstone and foundation on which to build is kingdom, He most certainly is choosing the right persons to complete the work of that kingdom. *"Having been built on the foundation of the apostles and prophets, Jesus Christ Himself being the chief cornerstone, in whom the whole building, being fitted together, grows into a holy temple in the Lord, in whom you also are being built together for a dwelling place of God in the Spirit"* (Ephesians 2:20-22) From this we can ascertain that when God has something He wants to build, He is very intentional and deliberate about the articles He chooses to use to accomplish it. Therefore, wherever He places us, it is according to His will, and His will is perfect, and we are perfectly suited for the thing or things He has for us to do. If He wants to use you, rest assured, He knows you can do it. The work of the kingdom is far too valuable, and the instruments far too critical, for God not to select those who will aid Him in completing the work and fulfilling the purpose correctly.

> *"But now God has set the members, each one of them,*
> *in the body just as He pleased."*

(I Corinthians 12:18)

Bring to Brought

In being overly preoccupied with his expression of reluctance and insecurity about the assignment God was giving him, Moses missed a very important statement of assurance God makes to him. It's found in Exodus 3:12. God in responding to Moses in this verse and speaks to Moses in the past tense, telling Moses what his plans are after completing the assignment of bringing the people out of Egypt. *"And this shall be a sign to you: <u>When you have brought</u> the people out of Egypt, you shall serve God on this mountain."* God, in an effort to assure Moses that he would succeed and build his confidence, says to him *"When you have brought..."* Look at how amazing that is. God is speaking as though Moses has already done it. He doesn't say, <u>if</u> you bring them out, or <u>if</u> you happen to be successful in bringing them out; no, He uses *"When"* and then He uses *"brought"*, which is the past indicative of <u>bring</u>. And there is no way you can have "brought" unless you have first been able to "bring." So God is virtually telling him, as far as I am concerned, when you go, if you go, it is already done. I just need you to go. God is guaranteeing him a win, but he can't see or hear it because he can't get past himself and see God. Similarly, we can miss God's assurances of our ability to complete whatever it is He is asking us to do and remain fearful and reluctant, bathing in tub of "But What If I Fail" and similar questions like it. When we fail to get past what we view as our limitations and inabilities and see God's hands at work in us and through us, we find there is not much God is able to accomplish through us. What things have you resisted when being asked by God to do, because you couldn't get past yourself and just see God the great I AM?

We can see evidence of Moses having completely missed God's effort to assure him he would be successful. In verse number one of the fourth chapter of Exodus, Moses responds back to God by saying: ***"But suppose they will not believe me or listen to my***

voice... " Moses responds in this manner after being guaranteed success. God, realizing that Moses was still not where he needed to be in order to leave for Egypt, in verses 2-9 of Exodus four, God takes Moses through an exercise of demonstrating to him ways in which He was going to work through him to get the job done. Aren't you glad that God, through His love, has such wonderful fatherly patience with us? He so often sees us where we are, and with patient care and divine nudging moves us to where we need to be. Praise God!

When the assignment, calling, position, role or purpose is from God, we must keep in mind that there are things that have been deposited in our very depths by Him that are undiscovered, they have not been extracted; because we have not yet moved forth into the assignment that will bring them to the surface. Furthermore, there may be skills we may have, or experience we possess, that God wants to use for His glory and for furtherance of His kingdom. Things that we may have never thought could be of any use to Him. Yet with His careful eye He has chosen to use them. As we feel drawn into doing something we have never done, we can be confident in the One who has assigned it to us, and press forward with confidence knowing that it's not our calling but His.

Chapter Four

Called To What?

I would like to again state that I do realize, and am certain, that not all of us are called to leadership, and of course not all called to impact millions of lives as Moses did. However, I am convinced that we are all called to something. Certainly, not everyone is called to be a pastor, preacher, minister, or evangelist, but we are all called or drawn by the Holy Spirit to influence and impact the areas within the Kingdom of God that have been assigned to us. *"There are diversities of gifts, but the same Spirit."* (I Corinthians 12:4) Not being a leader or minister, or someone who is very visible, does not give us an excuse or release us from the responsibility of impacting the lives and completing the work that we each individually have been charged by God to impact and complete. *"The manifestation of the Spirit is given to each one for the profit of all."* (I Corinthians 12:7)

Body Parts

The human body is a scientific and biological marvel. It is the most advanced and complex single organism on the entire plant, and the most magnificent of all God's creation. The human body consists of millions of cells, tissues, organs and extremities, all with different attributes and functions, working to address various needs. All of the different parts work together in unison, and together make up one body. This is true also of the *Body of Christ*, the global church-at-large. The Body of Christ consists of the born-again believers in Christ all over the world. *"Now you are the body of Christ, and members individually."* (I Corinthians 12:27) Although the human body is an earthly body, and the Body of Christ is a spiritual body, they both bear a resemblance to one another. Like the human body, the Body of Christ is comprised of various different parts, playing many roles and fulfilling many different purposes. Paul states this very clearly in I Corinthians 12:12 where he states: *"For as the body is one and has many members, but all the members of that one body being many, are one body, so also is Christ."* The human body is an efficient, effective working organism with every part serving a need and complementing the other parts. God, the divine designer of the human body, has also magnificently designed the body of Christ to work in the same way. *"But now God has set the members, each one of them, in the body just as He pleased."* (I Corinthians 12:18) Just as God has equipped the human body with all that it needs to live and thrive, He has also provided His Body in Christ with everything it needs to function and thrive in impacting this world for Him. As members of the Body of Christ, every person is necessary for the health and survival of the body, as well as to get the work of the body done, even as every part of the human body is necessary.

Serving Opportunities

*"There are differences of ministries, but the same Lord.
And there are diversities of activities, but it is the same
God who works all in all."*

(I Corinthians 12:5-6)

With careful consideration of the Body of Christ, which has the charge of building God's earthly kingdom (the kingdom that was begun by Jesus Christ during His earthly ministry), we can see our efforts in the building of that kingdom best defined through our service in the local church. Local churches essentially are the primary way in which the vast majority of members in the Body of Christ can serve in the body. In addition, there are extensions of the work of the local church, such as foreign missions, homeless outreaches, and special-needs urban and rural missions. It is the local churches who aspire to be bodies of believers, who are members of the Body of Christ, striving to do their part in the kingdom. Although there are a myriad of churches which function in various locations, all serving the work of the same kingdom. And while there are many professional skills and specialties that members of the local church bodies possess, many people who possess those skills have never considered them to be useful in the building of the kingdom. There again, in some cases, people have considered but have been reluctant to respond to God's calling and accept a new challenge.

Consider this suggestive list of areas in which God may desire to use skills obtained and perfected outside of the Body of Christ, to aid in the work within the body. The names of the different areas listed are generic, and the efforts of each are broad and are designed to provide some suggestion but not specific direction. Seeking guidance from the Holy Spirit and working with the pastor of your congregation is warranted.

Children & Youth Ministry

For those who love children and have a knack for explaining things or have instructional training, there are the possibilities of teaching in either children's church or Sunday school. Another option may be not actually teaching, but serving as a youth coordinator or youth director who works to support and organize the processes of teaching the children and youth. A customer service representative with a heart for young people, can volunteer and be a support to the youth pastor. There are options such as leading a youth bible study, or being a chaperon or volunteer for youth activities and outings.

Care Ministry

Those who have caring hearts and who are very thoughtful and considerate may find that they can be of great use serving in a care ministry and helping to visit the sick and elderly to offer prayer, or sending cards of concern, birthday and anniversary cards, or even offering support to those who are grieving or struggling with great life challenges. Arts and crafts hobbyists can create inspirational and encouraging keepsakes for the sad and heavy-hearted.

Church Operation, Administration, & Maintenance

Persons who are well organized and well planned may look for opportunities to serve as an assistant to the pastor, church secretary, or church office manager. An information technologist or I.T. specialist might work to develop and maintain the church's website, or oversee the purchasing of computers and office equipment, or help in the selection of software that manages the church's records, as well as training on the software. An accountant may offer assistance or advice in managing the church's financial records and bank accounts. A carpenter or handyman might help to identify ways in which some repairs and maintenance needs can be addressed at little to no cost. Managers and CEO's can help to organize church business processes to allow for more efficient operations. Team leaders can help to organize a group responsible for routine cleaning of the church. If fulfilled by church members, all of these service opportunities would help to reduce or in some cases eliminate professional services costs that the church would otherwise have to pay.

Music & Performing Arts Ministry

Past members of high school bands or teenage rock bands can now use those abilities as a part of the church Praise Band or Praise Orchestra. Childhood piano lessons can be used in serving as one of the church pianist or keyboardists. Singers, who have professional experience, or once had aspirations to sing professionally, or simply enjoy singing, can now serve as praise and worship leaders or become a part of and even help to direct the church choir, choral, or worship team. Dancers, where permitted, can develop or become a part of Praise Dance troops. Playwrights can write and direct inspirational stage plays and dramas that help to share the gospel message. Actors can perform as cast members for the plays. Funny men and women can serve as Christian Comedians, providing an added venue for Christian entertainment.

Hospitality Ministry

Persons with pleasant personalities and warm smiles can serve as greeters and ushers helping to welcome visitors and assist the physically challenged, or helping to host new members' receptions. Those who are fluent in the language of sign can serve as signers for the hearing impaired during worship services. Maintenance workers who have demonstrated faith and servanthood can serve as Deacons and Church Elders helping to visit the sick and those unable to attend worship services. Those who are fluent in foreign languages can help with translation of Christian development materials, or provide instruction on English as a second language.

Media Ministry

Disc jockeys and electronic buffs can serve to manage the sound during worship services, editing of compact disc and cassette tape originals for reproduction, offer advice and guidance on equipment needs and purchases, as well as potential upgrade requirements. Photographers can serve as camera technicians for video recording of worship services, video editing for reproduction, or develop a photography ministry within the church.

Special Events Ministry

Caterers can manage the church's kitchen or oversee food service during church fellowship dinners, events and receptions. Event coordinators can head planning committees for dinners, receptions and special celebrations. Home school moms can chair activities committees for annual community days and family days. Program managers can lead program development committees for special initiatives the church may have. Graphic designers can help to design fliers, posters and banners to promote church events.

Outreach, Evangelism & Spiritual Development

"Type A" personalities that never meet a stranger can serve by going door-to-door to take prayer requests and invite people to church. They can help to feed the homeless, help pass out plan of salvation tracts, call on lapsed members, or serve in prison ministries. Construction workers who have good instructional skills can teach new members' classes or lead bible study groups. Teachers and professors can help to develop curriculum for faith development classes.

All of these are functioning parts of the body of Christ. Like the human body, some parts are used more frequently, while others are used less frequently or only when needed, but all are important and intricate to God and to the kingdom work He has ascribed to the body of Christ to complete. Although the roles vary, the significance of the purpose remains the same throughout. *"There are differences of ministries, but the same Lord. And there are diversities of activities, but it is the same God who works all in all. "* (I Corinthians 12:5-6) With the many different ministry needs of our churches today, there are a vast number of ways in which one can serve in the kingdom of God.

"Having then gifts differing according to the grace that is given to us, let us use them."

(Romans 12:6)

Chapter Five

Why Am I Reluctant to Start?

It is a natural and instinctively human reaction to have fear. It is one of the many involuntary emotions that we as human beings possess and express.

Fear of Failing

Atychiphobia is a technical term used to describe the fear of failure or failing. It is further understood to be an extreme and irrational fear. Another term used to describe this condition is *Kakorrhaphiophobia*, which is the fear of failure also but includes the fear of defeat. I am certainly not suggesting that the vast majority of us suffer from either of these clinical conditions. I would, however, like to consider the basic element of fear that manifests in us in ways much less than that of a phobia, but that creates in us reluctance; the kind of reluctance that causes us to be reticent to try something new because we have never done it before.

Far too often we take the position of "wait and see" when we are faced with moving in a direction we have never gone before, or seeking to accomplish something that we have never accomplished before. We settle on waiting to see if the first step will some day get easier. It is a proven fact that when trying something new, the first step is the hardest step in the process. The problem with the "wait and see" approach is that if we never make the first step, we will never have a second, third, or even a fourth step. In these instances, we will essentially never know what could have been accomplished. How many things have remained undone because they are left waiting, collecting dust on the shelves of "wait and see?" Those things that we did not try or were unwilling to try that if we would have tried we may have done an exceptional job, or may have discovered an ability that we did not know existed.

Most of us can likely recall a childhood memory of something that did not go well for us, or maybe it's not something from your childhood but from teenage or young adult years. No matter at which point in our lives, it is safe to assume that we all have had an encounter with feelings of failure. Things we feel we messed up or didn't do very well. Because we have the ability to recall the feelings that we experienced as a result of an event, those feelings have the ability to affect us even much later in life. These feelings cause us to experience a heightened sense of anxiety when we feel we may encounter those feelings again. So our reluctance becomes a product of an effort to avoid the "feelings" we associate with failing. This is very similar to the instant response to heat, when we instantly draw back our hand, having recalled burning our finger at some point earlier in life. This can easily hamper our ability to say yes to an opportunity that God may present to us, even though we have the backing of God's word, which assures us that we can do all things through Christ who provides our strength, or enables us. (Philippians 4:13) This assurance is even heightened when we are committing ourselves to follow the will God has for our lives. If we become accustomed to defining our inability through our God-given abilities, and filter our failures through the strainer of God's word, we would come to realize that we possess greater aptitude than the things we have already done.

Moses too, at a younger age while still in Egypt, tried something that didn't work out like he planned and could even be considered something he failed in. Therefore, when God began to call him to go back to Egypt, he undoubtedly began to recall the experience. In Exodus 2, we find a younger Moses trying to <u>rescue</u> a fellow Hebrew who was being afflicted by an Egyptian. This didn't work out as he had planned and Moses eventually flees from Egypt when the Pharaoh at that time discovered his actions. *"When Pharaoh heard of this matter, he sought to kill Moses, But Moses fled from the face of Pharaoh and dwelt in the land of Midian; and he sat down by a well."* (Exodus 2:15) Then forty years later, in chapters three and four of Exodus, we find God commissioning Moses to go back to Egypt (the Pharaoh who sought to kill him was dead) to once again <u>rescue</u>, but this time not just one Hebrew man, but the entire Hebrew population in Egypt. It would seem that after having had the first rescue attempt turn sour, it would be only natural for Moses to wrestle with the question ***"But What If I Fail,"*** when God is now asking him to repeat the action, but in a different way and on a much larger scale. We find an example of this question surfacing in verse number one of the fourth chapter of Exodus. ***"Then Moses answered and said, But suppose they will not believe me or listen to my voice; suppose they say, The Lord has not appeared to you."*** According to modern estimates, there were approximately two million (some estimates are higher) Hebrew men, women and children in Egypt at the time of the exodus. These estimates are based a good part on the first census of the people God ordered in the first chapter of Numbers, which yielded a sum of 603,550 men not including the women and children. Unquestionably, Moses recalled that there was a large number of Hebrew people already in existence when he fled from Egypt some 40 years earlier (Acts 7:30), and now he was being asked to rescue all of them when he had not felt very successful after his first rescue attempt.

Fear Ridding Love

"In this the love of God was manifested toward us, that God has sent His only begotten Son into the world, that we might live through Him." (I John 4:9)

You or I, as partakers in the grace of God extended to us through Jesus Christ and made available to us because of His love, are not much different than Moses. We have most certainly had something, or things in our past that we did not succeed in. And those experiences no doubt caused us to experience feelings of failure and defeat, and deposited thoughts of reluctance that affect us even in cases where we believe God wants to use us. We are oftentimes sure we love God and are sure we want to be obedient to Him. We even have a desire to serve Him in some capacity, yet we are hampered by our fear. We fail to realize that it is through the perfect love God has for us, and the ever-perfecting love that we have for Him, that we are able to overcome our fear and adequately rid ourselves of the fear that holds us back. The fear that keeps us from submitting to the will of God to use us as His instrument, and the way in which He desires to use us. *"There is no fear in love; but perfect love casts out fear, because fear involves torment. But he who fears has not been made perfect in love."* (I John 4:18) It is through God's perfect love that we can even be considered as instruments in service to Him, and it is upon that perfect love we must rely, when our unperfected love still produces fear within us. The reluctance we have must be made subject to the demonstrated love God has for us. If we will only trust Him, and be confident in His love, God's perfect love will cast out the reluctant fear that may stir within us; that prohibits us from actively striving to accomplish in God the things He has set before us to complete.

Four Promises

As Moses wrestled with his fear, God makes some promises to him to encourage him, and to settle him. God first promises him that He would be with him. *"I will certainly be with you."* (Exodus 3:12) Then God promises Moses that He would work through him to complete the mission. *"Now therefore, go, and I will be with your mouth and teach you what you shall say."* (Exodus 4:12) God made these promises to Moses to assure him and increase his confidence, because no matter how empty his confidence tank may have been, he could fill it with God's promises. Just as God promised Moses when He desired to use him, God has promised us that He will be with us and lead us through whatever it is that He has called us to do.

"Fear not, for I am with you; Be not dismayed, for I am your God, I will strengthen you, Yes, I will help you, I will uphold you with My righteous right hand." (Isaiah 41:10)

What awesome words of comfort and assurance that we can use to encourage ourselves against fears of failing that cause us to be reluctant. There are four promises God makes in this verse, and we will consider each one. The first promise we find in this passage of scripture is: *"I am with you."* There is no greater comfort than to know that God Himself is with you in times of uncertainty, in times of doubt and confusion, or in times of fear and hesitation. Knowing that God will be there with us can bring about a calming peace even though a storm of fear may be raging. The second promise He makes is: *"I will strengthen you."* When trying to trail blaze through uncharted terrains in our life or in our service to the Lord, the fear of failure can zap all of our strength and cause us to want to give up and turn back and return to more familiar pastures. But the confidence we have is that when our strength has failed us, God has promised to strengthen us. The third promise we see in this passage is *"I will help you."* A little child while trying to unscrew the top off a glass jar may become frustrated and feel like she has failed and would not succeed. But just as she is about to give up, her father noticing that she would not be able to do it on her on, steps in and says "I will help you." We have the same awesome blessing of knowing that when we are unable to go it alone, our Heavenly Father will always step in and say, *"I will help you."* The fourth and final promise we see in this passage is: *"I will uphold you with My righteous right hand."* Many times once we have accepted that God wants to use us and we begin to walk in the assignment, we might find that it may not be easy to sustain as things seem to not be going as planned, and fearful feelings of failure begin to lurk. In those times, we have the faithful assurance that God has promised to uphold us with His righteous right hand. There is no better hand to be held by. *"My Father, who has given them to Me, is greater than all; and no one is able to snatch them out of My Father's hand."* (John 10:29)

One primary thing we must keep in mind when faced with feelings of the possibility of failing is that the difference when considering or preparing to do something for God, is God! He is the difference maker! This is expressed very clearly in II Corinthians 12:9 where we find these awesome words of comfort and assurance *"...My strength is made perfect in weakness."* In other words, God's ability is at its best in your inability. God's potential through you, empowers you with potential that is unmatched, undefeated and is unfailing. So in spite of your potential to fail, you will not fail because you are not operating based upon your potential but His potential, or your "God Potential."

Chapter Six

Too Little to Contribute

Oftentimes our fear of failure is bred in feelings of inadequacy, believing that we do have something to contribute, but feeling that what we have to contribute won't be enough, won't make a difference, or won't amount to very much. Moses had feelings very similar to these. He expressed this when he responded to the Lord with: *"O my Lord, please send by the hand of whomever else You may send."* (Exodus 4:13) He is suggesting to God that He didn't have very much to contribute, but that there has to be someone else that is better qualified and better prepared than he was. Paul tries to defuse this way of thinking in us when he describes the body of Christ and the significance of each member in the twelfth chapter of his first Epistle to the Corinthian church:

"For in fact the body is not one member but many. If the foot should say, 'Because I am not a hand, I am not of the body,' is it therefore not of the body? And if the ear should say, 'Because I am not an eye, I am not of the body,' is it therefore not of the body? If the whole body were an eye, where would be the hearing? If the whole body were hearing, where would be the smelling? But now God has set the members, each

one of them, in the body just as He pleased. And if they were all one member, where would the body be? But now indeed there are many members, yet one body. And the eye can not say to the hand, 'I have no need of you;' nor again the head to the feet, 'I have no need of you.'" (I Corinthians 12:14-21)

Through Paul, God is letting us know that every one of us has an important role to play. And that none of us can afford to not do the things that God would have us to do or has purposed for us to do. Notice how the foot desires to be the hand. Both the foot and the hand are used regularly, however, because the hand is more visible and is involved in more things, the foot wants to be the hand. Not being satisfied to complete his purpose, the foot is not realizing that his role of helping to carry the body is vitally important. The foot discounts the fact that he is a part of the foundation on which the entire body stands. For without the foot helping to carry the body, the whole body including the hand, would be limited in where it can go and what it can accomplish. Observe also how the ear is complaining: "I am sick of being around here on the side of the head. I want to be up front, no longer on sidelines or behind the scene. I want to be a part of the main show." The ear is desiring to be more noticeable, more recognizable, right in the middle of the action. When the ear desires to be the eye, he loses sight of how many times the body has depended on his unique and exclusive ability to hear in order to be alerted of danger, or has experienced the beauty of a symphony or a bird singing; something that no other part of the body can enable the body to do. Every part of the body has its own unique purpose and services its own specific need. As members of the body of Christ, it is imperative that we each recognize that our unique abilities, gifts, skills, talents, and experiences are all essential to the functioning of the whole body. God has positioned us where He feels we can best serve the body and therefore His kingdom.

"Whatsoever you do, do all to the glory of God"

(I Corinthians 10:31)

This verse of scripture provides us with so much perspective related to our contributions to the kingdom. When it comes to what we have to contribute, it really boils down to whether or not God is reaping glory and honor out of what we are doing. It is not important how large or small our contribution is, or how recognizable it is. What is imperative is that it is for God's glory, and His alone. He is not concerned with the size of the contribution; He is only concerned with the heart of the contribution.

The Heart Of The Gift

There is an illustration of how God views what we give to Him found in the twelfth chapter of Mark's gospel beginning at verse 41. In this scene, Jesus is sitting near the place where the people brought and deposited their offerings. He noticed how those who had much to give gave much, not out of the abundance of their heart, but out of the abundance of what they had to give. Then came along a widow, who offered what would be almost the equivalent of two pennies today. Jesus says this of her gift: *"Assuredly, I say to you that this poor widow has put in more than all those who have given to the treasury."* (Mark 12:43). Jesus' heart was moved by her gift, because she gave all she had to give. And although it didn't seem like much to the others sitting by watching, God knew the value of what she gave. There is an old statement I remember hearing since I was a child that states: *"What comes from the heart, reaches the heart."* There may be others who seem to have more to give because they have many gifts and talents, or they have greater access to resources than you. However, be encouraged to know that no matter what you have to offer the Lord, when it is given from your heart it will never be considered by God to be *"Too Little To Contribute."* It is not just a matter of *what* you give of yourself to the Lord; it is also *how* you give of yourself. When we serve God out of a committed heart, what we do pleases Him. It reaches His heart. If we are only willing to do things in the kingdom to be recognized or acknowledged, then the things that we are doing become tainted. They are like bruised fruit. The fruit may still have nutrients and vitamins that are a part of its natural make up, but it has lost some of its appeal. Jesus has this to say regarding doing things only for recognition: *"Moreover, when you fast, do not be like the hypocrites, with a sad countenance. For they disfigure their faces that they may appear to men to be fasting. Assuredly, I say to you, they have their reward."* (Matthew 6:16) From this we can conclude that when we do things for recognition, whatever acknowledgement or accolade people give us is all the benefit we will receive from it. Because in those cases, God didn't receive glory out of what we did and is therefore not pleased with what we did. The service that we offer to the kingdom should be for God and not for ourselves or for others.

"No, much rather, those members of the body which seem to be weaker are necessary. And those members of the body, which we think to be less honorable, on these we bestow greater honor."

(I Corinthians 12:22-23)

The Value of an Eyelash

Most of us will not place much significance on a single eyelash. However, when we consider that the primary function of our eyelashes is to help protect the eye, warning of any harmful foreign objects. Our eyelashes are like sensors. When an unwanted or unexpected object is traveling in the direction of the eye that may endanger the eye, and the eye has not seen the object, our eyelashes feel the presence of the unwelcome object and signal to the eyelid to immediately close. To emphasize, let's consider the eyelash in the outermost corner of the eye. It may have little significance in the day-to-day activity of the body. It may be the shortest, least appealing of all the rest of the lashes. Consider an object moving vigorously towards the eye that may cause damage to the eye. It is that small unattractive eyelash that is the first thing the object hits in route to the eye, and that eyelash immediately signals for the eyelid to close to protect the eye. That seemingly insignificant eyelash has become the most important part of the entire body at that moment. Many of us may feel as insignificant as that eyelash appeared to be, and may feel we have very little or nothing at all to contribute. However, just as the eyelash, when we have been called to a purpose, in fulfilling that purpose, we can very well be the most significant, most necessary, most appreciated part of the body at the time we are called forth to perform. That eyelash, whenever given an opportunity to accomplish its purpose, will always fulfill its purpose. It won't stop to consider how much smaller than the rest of the eyelashes it may be. It won't lose focus of its purpose sobbing about its positioning in the body. It won't become discouraged in its purpose and wishing that it was a different part of the body with a more significant purpose. It will not fail to do its part in protecting the eye just because it is not the eyelid. No it won't, it will do its job!

Focusing on our inabilities or being envious of others' abilities will always overshadow and hinder the discovery and fulfillment of our God-given abilities. This will cause us to become inactive, uninvolved and unmotivated. There are far too many members of the body of Christ that are MIA, (Missing In Action) because they have not realized that the purpose God has for them and the area in which God wants to use them is vitally important to the daily functioning of the Body of Christ. Just as the human body is designed to work together in unity, so is the body of Christ. Every part is of the body is necessary, from the eyelash to the toenail. When the eye has something in it, it needs the hand to remove it. When the hand is trying to write, it needs the eye to provide the vision to know where to write. When the leg needs to bend, it calls on the knee. When the back has an itch, it needs a scratch from the fingernail. Before the mouth gets its taste, it calls on the nose to give it a foretaste. Whatever part of the body of Christ you may be, what you have to contribute is necessary. Each individual part performing its responsibility is how the work gets accomplished, it's how the work of the kingdom gets done. Whatever you have to contribute, rest assured it is not too little.

"*And the eye cannot say of the hand, 'I have no need of you,' nor again the head to the feet, 'I have no need of you.' No, much rather, those members of the body which seem weaker are necessary.*" (I Corinthians 12:20-21)

Chapter Seven

Trust Factor

Generally speaking, the more you know someone, the more you trust that person. If you kind of know someone, then you are likely to kind of trust him or her. And if you really know someone then you are more likely to really trust him or her. When God desired to use Moses, He wanted Moses to get to know Him better, in order that he might better trust Him.

A Matter of Trust

In Exodus chapter 3, when God calls to Moses from the burning bush, after having commanded him to take off his sandals because the ground he was standing on was holy, God began helping Moses become better acquainted with Him. *"I am the God of your father, the God of Abraham- the God of Isaac, and the God of Jacob."* (Exodus 3:6) God then describes to Moses why He is now talking with him: *"I have surely seen the oppression of My people who are in Egypt, and have heard their cry because of their taskmasters, for I know their sorrows. So I have come down to deliver them out of the hand of the Egyptians, and bring them up from that land to a good and large land, to a land flowing with milk and honey, to the place of the Canaanites and the Hittites and the Amorites and the Perizzites and the Hivites and the Jebusites."* (Exodus 3:7-8) In describing to Moses His intentions, God is also allowing Moses to become better acquainted with His compassion and commitment to His people, and catch a glimpse of His character and consistency. God shows Moses His compassion when says to him: *"I know their sorrows,"* His commitment when He says: *"I have seen the oppression of My people who are in Egypt, and have heard their cry"*, His character when He said: *"So I have come down to deliver them out of the hand of the Egyptians,"* and His consistency when He reveals: *" I am the God of your father- the God of Abraham, the God of Isaac, and the God of Jacob."* It is in becoming better acquainted with God's character, compassion, commitment and consistency that we are able to better trust Him.

In Lamentations the third chapter, the prophet Jeremiah helps us to see this, as he expresses the hope (trust) he had in God, as a result of his experiences of God not failing him, nor allowing him to ever be overwhelmed in difficult times. *"This I recall to my mind, Therefore I have hope. Through the Lord's mercies we are not consumed, Because His compassions fail not. They are new every morning; Great is Your faithfulness."* (Lamentations 3:21-23) From Jeremiah's example, we can conclude that trust is a result of experience; experiencing God through actively becoming acquainted with Him. The most effective way of doing this is through the study, learning, and daily application of God's word in our lives. As we apply the principles of God's word in our lives, we cultivate experiences as a result of trusting God enough to put His word to the test, and those experiences in turn serve notice that we can trust Him again. *"For whatsoever things were written aforetime were written for our learning, that we through patience and comfort of the scriptures might have hope."* (Romans 15:4 - KJV) The Greek word translated into hope in this passage of scripture is *elpis,* which also means to have confidence. God's word teaches us about Him and His ways, it develops character in us through our understanding by helping us to exercise patience, and it comforts us by the assurance we receive from it. This all works together to develop our trust or confidence in God.

It would have been impossible for Moses to grasp enough of who God was during his initial encounter, thus we notice that as God reveals Himself more and more to Moses, over time Moses begins to trust Him more and more. It is after God reveals His name to Moses, assures Moses that He will be with him and working in him, demonstrates His power to Him, and later performs great miracles through Moses and His brother Aaron, that we find Moses' confidence and trust developing and growing in God, and His ability to use him. In like manner with you and I, increasing our trust of God requires our increasing our knowledge of Him, and increased trust in Him only happens when we grow to know and love Him more and more each day. Growing in our knowledge of God is not automatic because we attend church services. Rather, it is an active, ongoing, intentional process that requires our true desire and commitment. By then putting the things we learn of Him to the test and trusting Him in smaller things, we gradually increase our trust and are willing to trust God with what we feel to be the larger and more important aspects of our lives. To accomplish great things in God, it will require us to develop great trust in Him.

Just Trust In Me

In Exodus 3:11 Moses asks God the question: *"Who am I that I should go to Pharaoh, and that I should bring the children of Israel out of Egypt?"* God responds, *"I will certainly be with you..."* (Exodus 3:12) seems to say "Just trust in Me." Furthermore, as we examine the story of Moses, we find that Moses' preoccupation with asking what ultimately boils down to the proverbial question **"But What If I fail?"** seems to consistently cause him to miss God's resolute answer: "Just trust in Me." Let us look a little further into the story to observe this. We have already noted above Moses' initial response to God's request to use him. We now see Moses again expressing his unwillingness in Exodus 4:1 as Moses asks: *"But suppose they will not believe me or listen to my voice..."* and God responds in verses two through nine of chapter four explaining and demonstrating to Moses how He was going to be with him through signs and wonders. This again amounts to God saying "Just trust in Me." Once again Moses expresses his reluctance in Exodus 4:10 by stating: *"Oh my Lord, I am not eloquent, neither before nor since You have spoken to Your servant; but I am slow of speech and slow of tongue."* And God again responds with "Just trust in Me" when He states in Exodus 4:12 *"Now therefore, go, and I will be with your mouth and teach you what you shall say."*

This same scenario plays out in our daily lives as well. We are at times more focused on failures and lack of ability, faithfully cataloging them and busily indulging our fear of failure, that we close our ears to hearing God saying to us "Just trust in Me." How many times has God desired to use us to share the gospel message with an unbelieving co-worker or friend, and we decided not to because we began thinking of all the things we didn't know or couldn't explain. We did not trust God to provide us the words. We did not trust Him to recall experiences we have had and remembrances of the things we do know that may help to bring that person into a relationship with the Lord Jesus Christ. There are individuals out there that will hear your voice. They may have had others share Christ with them, but there is something about your voice, your style, and your approach that they can relate to which allows them to hear the message in such a way or at such a point in their lives that they can accept it. God is saying to you, just as He said to Moses: *"I will be with your mouth and teach you what you shall say."* He simply needs you to trust Him to do just that.

> *"Trust in the Lord with all you heart,*
> *And lean not on your own understanding."*
>
> (Proverbs 3:5)

Each time Moses responded to God in this dialogue we find that he was focusing solely on himself and his ability, or lack thereof, as opposed to focusing on God's ability. In these instances, Moses was trusting only in his own finite understanding, and in doing so he was failing to place his confidence in God's infinite wisdom. Paraphrased, God reassures Moses that "I will be there with You," but Moses seems to respond with ***"But What If I Fail?"*** God says, "but I will be there using you," and Moses continues to ask ***"But What If I Fail?"*** Throughout this entire exchange God seems to state with all confidence and self-assurance "Trust Me, I don't fail" because "I AM, WHO I AM." God has never failed and never will. The perfect God had a perfect plan, and was

51

choosing an imperfect vessel, and was telling the imperfect vessel, "I won't fail in you," because His strength or ability is perfected in our weakness or inability. (2 Corinthians 12:9)

This scene shows the infinitely wise and all knowing God, whose reasoning surpasses all human understanding, making a choice to use Moses to free His people from Egypt. However, Moses, in his finite understanding of God, is trying to convince God that He is making a bad decision. The problem here is that Moses is not picking up on the fact that he, with his limited human understanding and knowledge, was in no position to advise God, who is infinite in wisdom, and who has an unmatched amount of knowledge and understanding. *For who has known the mind of the Lord that he may instruct Him?* (I Corinthians 2:16) So even though we might say, "but God, I have never done it before," or "God I am not sure I can do it," He says to us as He said to Moses "I AM, WHO I AM," just Trust Me.

Chapter Eight

Settling Too Soon

Increasingly we are becoming a society of quitters. Many of us give up at the first sign of struggle or adversity, seeking only comfort and convenience, but all the while missing out on many opportunities to do something great, or accomplish something we have never before accomplished. The effects of this societal shift have, in turn, affected our churches and the kingdom work of the Body of Christ. So many members of the Body of Christ are increasingly only willing to serve in the local church when it is convenient. Or perhaps when agreeing to serve, we are only willing to serve on a limited basis for a very limited time. The problem with this is that now the local churches, and consequently the Body of Christ, have become what I would call paraplegic or quadriplegic. It is generally accepted, and my own personal observations and experiences would agree, that only a moderate percentage of the members in a given local church are doing 100% of the work in that church. Therefore, collectively the Body of Christ is functioning to complete the kingdom work, which requires the entire body, with only a portion of the body at work. This lack of effort by a large percentage of the Church of God, the Body of Christ, leaves the church disabled and handicapped, and limited in its ability to affect the world for Christ.

After Moses fled from Egypt and found a place where he felt comfortable and began performing an occupation in which he felt comfortable, it seemed that he would remain there and live the rest of his life as a shepherd of sheep. But as we know, that place was not Moses' destiny, nor was it the place God had purposed for him to remain. Moses had become settled without having reached the place God had intended for him and without having accomplished the things God had intended for him to do. In this chapter, we want to redirect our attention and draw from the experiences of Abraham, another well-known biblical figure. We will also include a brief look at his father.

Abram, who later became Abraham, was called by God to leave his familiar place in order that God could make him a father of many nations. God's calling required that Abram move in a direction that he had never gone in, to accomplish something he would have never accomplished without being willing to make the first step.

Terah

First let us look at Abram's father, Terah. We understand from Genesis 11:31 that it was Terah, Abram's father, who began the pilgrimage from the land of Ur to the land of Canaan. However, instead of completing the journey, he settled and died in Haran. *"And Terah took his son Abram, and his grandson Lot, and his daughter-in-law Sarai, his son Abram's wife, and they went out with them from Ur of the Chaldeans to go to the land of Canaan; and they came to Haran and dwelt there."*

We see here an example in which Terah settled too soon. Canaan was the original destination not Haran, but Haran became his destination. As with Terah, we oftentimes find ourselves after first hesitating to begin on an un-traveled path God has set for us, settling before accomplishing what God had intended because we become weary or because we look to find that which is familiar to us and stay there. History tells us that Haran, like Ur, was a center of the worship of the moon-goddess Nanna. So we can assume there may have been familiar surroundings, similar groups of people, similar buildings and structures, and even familiar daily activities. It would seem that this could have been an important factor as to why Haran was an appealing place for Terah to settle. Or maybe the journey from Ur to Haran was difficult, and figuring that the remainder of the route to Canaan would be just as difficult or worse, he decided to settle. We can't be certain either way, but what we do know is that he set out with his family for Canaan, but stopped and stayed in Haran. As human beings, we are creatures of habit and much prefer the familiar. Unfortunately, familiarity a great deal of the time will causes us to settle too soon when it comes to God's leading us in ways that are unfamiliar to us. There is essentially a collision that occurs between our trusting God, and our fear of the unknown. Because the unknown could include failing, we retreat back to more familiar surroundings or stop short of God's intended purpose. We are more willing to walk by sight rather than walk by faith, as we are instructed to do in I Corinthians 5:7, only going to a certain point, even though we have not completed our journey. We oftentimes proceed only to the point where we once again feel comfortable and familiar, and then we stop and stay. We are also very similar to water in this way, for as with water, we frequently settle for traveling the path of least resistance. This raises a few questions I'd like to pose: How many times have we been on a faith path and only travel so far and settled? How many places in our life or our walk with Christ have we reached and settled and will die there unless we move on? How many Harans are we living in right now? How many Canaans have we not reached? God is a master of stretching and expanding us, and taking us beyond what seems possible. On the other hand, we are masters of stopping and staying in familiar places; having reluctance and objections to stretching and expanding. We prefer to not go beyond the things we know to be possible through our own experiences or the experiences of others. God has thoughts and plans for us that exceed our expectations, and even in many cases don't resemble anything we have achieved before. However, unless we are willing to follow His plan to the end, we will never know all that God has planned for our lives. The words of God through the prophet Jeremiah seem to state this best:

"For I know the thoughts that I think toward you, says the Lord, thoughts of peace and not of evil, to give you a future and a hope."

(Jeremiah 29:11)

Canaan, in this case, represents the place of unfamiliarity, that we as believers are oftentimes faced with when we are charged by God to leave our place of comfort and fluency and move to a place that He desires for us to be; or doing of something in Him that we have never done before. Haran represents our staying in places in our lives that are short of what God has intended, or our faith paths with God that have ended short of the destination. Haran can also represent our continuing to only do things we are most comfortable with, or in some cases things we have found complacency in, because those places and things fit within our 'zone of conformability.'

Abraham

It would appear that Abram, like his father Terah, was also in danger of settling too soon and stopping short of reaching the place God had intended for him, possibly not accomplishing the things God had assigned to him. We see in the story that Abram remained in Haran for quite some time before leaving for Canaan. It wasn't until after his father's death that he then journeyed on to Canaan. One other observation I would like bring into this context would be what Stephen stated just before he was martyred in the book of Acts about Abraham, (Abram as his name wasn't changed to Abraham until later). He states that God had spoken to Abram before he settled in Haran and told him He wanted him to leave his country and his family and go to a land that He would show him. *"And he said, Brethren and fathers, listen: The God of glory appeared to our father Abraham when he was in Mesopotamia, before he dwelt in Haran, and said to him, Get out of your country and from your relatives, and come to a land that I will show you."* (Acts 7:2-3) I believe that from this we can suggest, with some degree of confidence, that Abram may have been the source of the prompting of his father Terah leaving Ur for Canaan. We don't find anywhere in scripture where Terah was told to go to Canaan or leave Ur, only Abram. There is only the record of Terah having set out for Canaan taking with him Abram, Sarai and Lot, but settled in Haran.

Abram was initially told by God to leave his country and family, but he did neither. And I believe that just like Moses, taking the first step for Abram wasn't easy either. I'd venture to say that even his succeeding steps were not easy, but he did not give up and settle too soon. He followed his father to Haran and stayed there with him until his death. Although he did delay in traveling the path God had for his life, Abram still completed the journey God had given him instructions to travel. It seems that many of us, however, do as Terah did and settle too soon, settling in our Haran which is short of the goal of our Canaan. If Abram had settled too soon, it's quite clear that he would have never become the great leader and legend of faith that he is today who bears the title of "Father of Many Nations." Through Abram continuing to follow and trust God, God continued to develop his faith to the point that Abram could believe that God could give him a son in his old age. Abram (Abraham) is now one of the benchmarks by which we as believers can measure our faith and trust in God. Settling too soon is not a successful exercise in faith, but a casualty of fear and doubt.

In order for Abram to continue to grow his faith enough to believe that God could do something unimaginable through him, Abram had to continue to travel the path God had for him. At the point when Abram leaves Haran, God has only told him that He was going to make him a great nation, but has not told him He would make him a great nation through a natural born son from Sarai his wife.

"Now the Lord had said to Abram: 'Get out of your country, From your family And from your father's house, To a land that I will show you. I will make you a great nation; I will bless you And make your name great; And you shall be a blessing. I will bless those who bless you, And I will curse him who curses you; And in you all the families of the earth shall be blessed.' So Abram departed as the Lord had spoken to him, and Lot went with him. And Abram was seventy-five years old when he departed from Haran." (Genesis 12:1-4)

It wasn't until he had traveled to where God was sending him, and continued in obedience, that God tells him that He would give him a son. Abram was 75 years old when he left Haran, but it wasn't until he was 99 years of age (Genesis 17:1) that God tells him Sarai would conceive a child in old age. During these 24 years Abram had patiently trusted God a little bit more each day. *"Knowing that the testing of your faith produces patience. But let patience have its perfect work, that you may be perfect and complete, lacking nothing."* (James 1:3-4) In doing so, his faith was perfected enough and complete enough to believe God to be able to give him a son through his wife Sarai, and cause him to become the "Father of Many Nations" (his name is changed to Abraham and Sarai's name is changed to Sarah). Had he not been willing to submit to what God desired to do through him, he would have never risen to the place that he did in God. Once we have made the first step in accepting that God wants to use us, we need to maintain a daily posture of trust in order that we can follow God's calling to the end and see the benefits of our obedience to Him. Although we may be faced with wanting to give up and settle too soon, if we remind ourselves daily that we must trust in Him and His calling of us, we will be strengthened to continue on. *"And let us not grow weary while doing good, for in due season we shall reap if we do not lose heart."* (Galatians 6:9) Abraham's example shows us that even though we may delay our going, and even at some point may pause in our going, if we conceive that the blessings of God for us, and works of God through us are only accomplished in our not settling too soon, then we will continue on to complete our purpose.

Chapter 9

Taking the First Step

Let's face it, when it comes to doing something we have never done, the first step is always the most difficult step to make. We will very often agonizingly consider all of the possible things that could go wrong or not come together to make whatever it is a success. We will ponder the likelihood of a failed outcome and even imagine in some cases how we will feel if we have an unsuccessful outcome. However, whenever God is requesting to use our time, talent, and our person, in order for Him to use us we must take the first step, and that is accept that God wants to use us.

Let's consider for a moment what the outcome would have been if Moses would have never taken the first step. What if after God called Moses, gave him instructions, assured him that He would be with him, that He would speak through him, and even gave him some support by allowing Aaron, his brother, to go with him, Moses still didn't go. One main conclusion we can draw from this is that he may have never gone back into Egypt, and would not have become the great leader of Israel that he became. He probably would have continued to tend his father-in-law's sheep, and maybe one day have sheep of his own, but ultimately not fulfilling the things that God had assigned to his hands to complete. The word of God assures us in Psalm 37:23 that the steps of a good man are ordered, directed or planned by the Lord. Here we have God giving Moses the order for his steps, and Moses is rebelling against God's plans, because he has determined within himself that the path God has chosen for him does not align with the expected path he conceived for his life. Isn't it so very typical for us to feel that way? I will later in this chapter discuss a similar experience of my own. Therefore, Moses is afraid to make even the first step. We are often reluctant to make the first step because we are too preoccupied with the possibility of our failing in the end. This way of thinking can be disastrous to our faith, because in this way of thinking the beginning is undermined by the possibility of a failed end. In fact, it is more productive that the beginning be inspired by the assurance we have from God's word in Philippians 4:13: *"I Can do all things through Christ who strengthens me."* When it comes to God's calling of us, or His expressed desire to use us, the prerequisite for making the first step is simply trusting God. Trusting that He already knows the end as well as the beginning, and with having that knowledge He is still choosing you. God chooses to use imperfect people in the fulfilling of His perfect plan. This is an amazing realization to grasp; that God knows that I have failed in the past, and He knows that I still have the capacity or potential to fail again, and yet He is still willing to take a chance on using me. He knows that I may not have full confidence in my abilities, He also knows that my human instinct is to be afraid of the unknown; yet He still desires to use me. If Moses in his rebutting conversation with God had realized this early on in the conversation, that God was consequently asking him to just trust Him, the conversation would have gone much differently, and would have been much shorter. In those times when we are faced with God's request to use us, if we begin with trusting God, we will find that allowing God to use us will become so much easier.

God's Calling Me?

When I felt God calling me into ministry, I was a Moses. I was in my final year of college, and had been praying for about eight months: "Lord, I know there are some things You want me to do, but I know it doesn't include preaching, so just show me what You want me to do and I'll do it." Notice that I had identified in my prayer what God was calling me to, but because I couldn't see myself doing it, or did not believe that I would do well at it, I ultimately was asking the preverbal question, ***"But What If I Fail,"*** just at Moses did. You see, I had never imagined myself as a minister of the gospel.

One Friday night God grabbed my attention. Someone who did not know that I had been praying this prayer for eight months, and who had only met me a couple days earlier, asked if I would deliver the sermon during a Sunday morning worship service. My immediate response was: "I'm not a preacher." The response back to me was: "The Lord told me to ask you." Now, I normally am not moved simply because someone says to me "God told me," or "God said." Rather, I always seek to search things out and try them by the Holy Spirit as John instructs us to do in I John 4:1, but there was something different about this time because I somehow knew God had said it. So I hesitantly responded back with "If the Lord told you to ask me then I guess I will have to come up with something, but it may not be much." That night I could think of nothing else. I could no longer casually pray about it. Then it hit me, "Oh my God, I am actually going to speak to a church congregation, on a Sunday morning!" My heart began to pound as I began thinking: "What am I going to do? I don't know how to preach. What will I say? Will what have to say make sense to anyone? Will I make a fool of myself?" In other words, ***"But What If I Fail?"***

At this point, I began praying more earnestly to God for direction. I believed that I was sufficiently busy doing my part in God's kingdom already. At the time, I was in my third year of leading a young men's ministry I had started in my church, was in my third year as President of my University's Gospel Choir, and was helping out at a another small church every other weekend. Seeking some guidance, I scheduled a meeting with my pastor to speak with him about my dilemma. I shared with him that I felt God may be calling me to preach, and that I had come to him for confirmation, hoping that God had told him the same thing, but his response shocked me. He said to me, "Son, if God is calling you to do something, it is not for me to know, it is for you to know and we will know based upon what you do." I sat back in my seat. I was dazed. I was stunned. I thought for sure if God wanted to use me in this way, undoubtedly He would have conferred with the man that I respected and admired the most. God later revealed to me that if my pastor, who was also my uncle, would have said to me, "Yes, I know, God told me you would be a preacher," because of my love and admiration for him I would have gone forth preaching based upon his words to me, rather than my having heard and found assurances in the call of God and responded in obedience to Him.

Now I was really desperate! Things hadn't gotten any easier, they seemed even harder now. As I drove back to college that evening I was anxious, uneasy and nervous. This idea of preaching just didn't sit well with me, and I was set against the idea. I began telling myself, "People expect preachers to wear suits; well I don't have any suits, I don't even like suits." I also agonized thinking, "Preachers have to stand in front of groups of people, and I hate standing in front of groups of people, I get nervous, my hands sweat profusely, and my heart races when I am in front of a group." So I was convinced this could not be what God was requiring of me, although it was becoming clear to me that it was. So I continued to sincerely pray for guidance.

Not long after this, God spoke to me while in prayer and said to me, "It's not whether or not I'm calling you, it's whether or not you are accepting." Tears began to run down my face and fear began to stir within, because I knew that I had a decision to make and that decision required me to take the first step, to accept that God wanted to use me in a way that I had never been used before to do something I never imagined I could do. My tearful response to Him was, "Lord here I am, I'm willing." This was the beginning of my trust of Him in a way I had never trusted Him before, to do something I had never done before. With confidence I can say that if I would have never been willing to take the first step and simply accept that God wanted to use me, I am certain I would not be writing this book, have been used in the ways God has used me, nor would I have impacted the lives that God has used me to influence over the years.

I must say, that request for me to speak on a Sunday morning, due to some scheduling changes, never did happen. However, the idea of it was just the right vehicle for God to get my attention, and cause me to sincerely seek to know what His purpose was for my life. For it was the urgency that I felt that night that stirred my heart's conviction, and awakened in me something that had been lying dormant; something I didn't know even existed.

Like Moses, I had my rebuttals and my arguments as to why God's choosing of me was not the right choice; also like Moses, I did accept. *"So Moses went and returned to Jethro his father-in-law, and said to him, 'Please let me go and return to my brethren who are in Egypt, and see whether they are still alive.' And Jethro said to Moses, 'Go in peace.'"* (Exodus 4:18) Moses became the great leader and accomplished all the wonderful things he did for God, because he was willing to take the first step and accept God's call to serve. If God desires to use you, you too will have to make the first step and accept that He wants to use you.

Chapter Ten

Pitiful Me

A simple breakdown of the word pitiful yields a compound usage of part of two primary words pity and full. If we reverse the position of the two words, we come up with "full of pity." Pity is a great adversary to faith. Pity has regret, and is born out of failure or disappointment in things that pertain to us. Faith, on the other hand, is the manifestation of things that pertain to God and His ability. Ephesians 3:20 states, *"Now to Him that is able to do exceedingly abundantly above all we ask or think, according to the power that works in us."* Self-pity due to failures is outmatched when it is set against the boundless abilities of our God. When we take the pity we feel because of past failures and disappointments, and drape it with confidence in our almighty God, we will find that we will feel a greater sense of empowerment, and experience higher levels of accomplishment from day-to-day.

The Faith Factor

Having faith is trusting even when there is nothing visible to trust in. *"Now faith is the substances of things hoped for, the evidence of things not seen."* (Hebrews 11:1) Faith is maintaining confidence in something even though you don't see it right now, believing that you will see it. You may not visibly see in yourself the abilities that would be required to do the things God is calling you to do, but faith is having confidence in Him. Having confidence in the fact that He is calling you to do something should begin to boost confidence in you. Realizing how important the Kingdom work is to God, He would not select someone that would not be an asset to the work He is trying to complete. If we are going to do anything for God, it is going to require some faith. We realize this through the profound and sobering statement made in the eleventh chapter of Hebrews verse six: *"But without faith it is impossible to please Him, for he who comes to God must believe that He is, and that He is a rewarder of those who diligently seek Him."* God's benefits package has great rewards and bonuses, however the work requires merits of faith.

Just like any potential employer, after receiving your application or resume, they want to interview you to determine if you will be an asset to the company. The employer would want to know if hiring you would help to improve the company's performance. In like manner, when God is hiring for *"Kingdom Inc."*, He is looking to enlist help that He has determined will be an asset to His company. He is looking to hire those who will improve His company's performance. If you fear failure, rest reassured that God would not be seeking to hire your services unless He was certain that you would be an asset to His workforce.

More often than not we are laden with self-pity because we have become preprogrammed for pity due to failed efforts in our past. Moses, because of his failure in his earlier attempts to rescue one Israelite from the hand of one Egyptian, had become preprogrammed in pity, and was greatly opposed to the idea of rescuing the entire nation of Israel from all of Egypt. When we become programmed for pity, we find that we are not only reluctant to pursue unknown possibilities based on fear, but that our reluctance is also a result of our own self-pity due to past failures and disappointments.

Shut Down the Party

Moses' stark objections to God's desire to use him seem to suggest that after fleeing Egypt, in addition to tending sheep on the back side of the mountain, Moses may have spent a great deal of time planning and hosting a pretty major one-man pity party. You know, the type of party that requires only one attendee in order for it to be a success, and can last for days, months, or even years.

After my first year in college, I transferred to another university, hoping that I would get a fresh start in a new environment. At the end of my first year at the new university, I discovered that I had only a 1.6 cumulative grade point average. Although I use the term discovered, it was not discovery. Nor was it some major surprise that hit me all of a sudden. I knew I had not applied myself adequately. On the other hand, I did feel I had done a little better than what my grades reflected. I was placed on academic probation, and was in jeopardy of being dismissed from school, or losing the financial aid (scholarships, grants, and loans) that I so desperately needed to remain in school, or both. I was devastated. The idea of failing in my attempt to earn a college degree greatly disturbed me, and I was embarrassed to discuss it with my parents. At that point, I considered dropping out and getting a full-time job, but that idea didn't sit very well with me. That summer, I was feeling pretty sorry for myself, blaming my high school teachers for not better preparing me for college, and even citing that no one in my immediate family had completed college, and that financially I was barely able to be in school in the first place. I was now the host and honored guest of one major pity party. The problem, in this case, wasn't my inability to do the work, but my lack of putting forth the effort to get the work done. I had not committed myself to my studies, nor had I prepared adequately for my exams.

I decided that I was going to go back to school and give it my best effort. However, at that point, I also had a head-on collision with the haunting question: ***But What If I Fail?*** "What if I give my best effort and the outcome is not much different?" I hadn't done so well up to this point, and furthermore in my mind I had already failed. Now I was faced with the question as to whether or not giving it another shot would end in the same way. Feeling a little deflated, I began praying. I asked God if I would give my best effort, would He help me to complete all of my course work and earn my degree. As I mentioned before, I was able to understand my course work, but my inability or lacks were in my study habits and lack of focus on my studies. I had failed as a high school student to develop study patterns that would foster better grades in college. Notice that I didn't pray, "God, give me better grades," or "God, give me my college degree." No, because if God were to give me grades and a degree that I had not worked for, He would not be helping me and would only be enabling my failed behavior and patterns. Therefore, my prayer was for God to help me to do the things that I needed to do and accomplish. When we solicit His help through prayer, He is able to make up the difference. As in this case, I didn't lack ability; I lacked positive study skills and discipline to adequately focus on schoolwork. Thus, in praying and asking God for guidance, and being willing to submit to His guidance, God was able to begin directing me toward better self-discipline with regard to studying. I began to see that through my submission to God, He was also building me in other areas where I was lacking.

After praying, I felt an assurance that my success would not hinge solely on my ability, but it would include the help of my God. With this newfound confidence, I then began to set my sights on doing something I had never done before, earn a place on the Dean's Academic Achievement List. After shutting down my pity party, I solicited God's help and guidance, and then I expanded my expectations. I began committing time in the library to study and prepare for classes. I completed all of the assigned work and attended every class session. I then adopted a habit of prayer; a simple prayer before each one of my exams, "Lord, help me to have clarity in my thoughts, help me to not become overwhelmed with nervousness, and bring back to my remembrance the things that I have studied and heard in the lectures, in Jesus' name, Amen." I am very proud to say that after three semesters, with God's help I made the Dean's List. Furthermore, because of the academic turnaround, I was recommended and accepted to the National Dean's List my senior year. Glory be to God! If I had allowed myself to remain "full of pity," slow-dancing with myself at my exclusive one-man pity party, I would have never trusted God to help me turn things around. Nor would I have been willing to take the steps that brought about the change and desired end. I didn't know in the beginning that God was going to use me to bring glory and honor to Himself. Since that time, I have shared this testimony with many individuals. I use this past experience as an instrument to encourage people to believe that with God working through us, we can accomplish things we never thought were possible. And for them to be willing to face the unknown, knowing that if God is with you He can make all the difference in the world. I certainly would have never known this for myself if I would have remained in my thinking of "Pitiful Me."

Adam

How often has God desired or presented an opportunity before us in which He would receive glory and honor through us, and He has been hindered because of our pre-orientation to pity. When God created us in the likeness of His image, because we bore his likeness we were not programmed to pity ourselves. If we consider the first man, Adam, in the second chapter of Genesis, we find that he was originally not aware of pity. For it is God who realizes that he was alone, and God who says that it is not good for man to be alone. (Genesis 2:18) To this point, Adam had been busy doing the things God had given him to do, and had a track record of success. So Adam was not sitting around in self-pity and complaining that there were no other creations like him and how alone he felt because of it. However, after his failure, we see that Adam becomes reprogrammed from his original God-given preprogrammed state of mind. Subsequent to this reprogramming, we find him making a statement to God that exhibits a "pitiful me" attitude. After he and Eve had failed by not keeping God's commandment, by eating from the tree of the knowledge of good and evil, which they had been forbidden to do (Genesis 2:17), we now find Adam making this statement, *"Then the man said, 'The woman whom You gave to be with me, she gave me of the tree, and I ate.'"* (Genesis 3:12)

Because we have all experienced failure in our lives, we have the ability to become pitiful in areas of our lives, and more specifically when it comes to God's desire to use us in His kingdom. As we can see from this example, even things that are a blessing to us can become viewed negatively when we become oriented to pity. Initially Adam was excited and blessed to have Eve, for he joyfully proclaims, *"This is now bone of my bones and flesh of my flesh; She shall be called Woman, Because she was taken out of Man."* (Exodus 2:23) But his view changed when is he started wearing the garments of self-pity. For then he exclaims, *"The woman who You gave to be with me, she gave me of the tree, and I ate."* (Exodus 3:12) Consequently, our failures can cause us to not recognize the blessing and privilege of God's desire to use us, but can cause us to view His calling of us negatively with fear and hesitation. Not acknowledging the honor and esteem associated with being an instrument in the hands of the Almighty God.

Thus Moses should have identified the awesomeness of having the God of the universe, Creator of all things, including him, requesting him to be His instrument of deliverance to His chosen people. However, because of his pitiful positioning, he is reluctant and even is opposed to a great and magnificent opportunity. Thankfully, he finally yielded to what God had called him to do. When God desires to use us, it should always be considered a blessing and viewed as a privilege. Sometimes though, self-pity can be an obstacle and cause us not to see God's calling in that light. We have to be deprogrammed from self-pity due to failures and become reprogrammed to our original preprogrammed state of trusting in our God to be able to work through us even though we have failed in the past.

Chapter Eleven

I Can, You Can

"I will certainly be with you. And this shall be a sign to you that I have sent you: When you have brought the people out of Egypt, you shall serve God on this mountain."

(Exodus 3:12)

"Now to Him who is able to do exceedingly abundantly above all that we ask or think, according to the power that works in us."

(Ephesians 3:20)

The God we serve is "A Great God Who Does Great Things," and He wants to use us in order to do something great in us and something great through us. He specializes in greatness. Notice in the above verse one simple phrase: "is able to do." Our God is a Doer. He gets things done. And everything He does is great! When He does, He exceeds ("exceedingly") expectations, He exceeds understanding, He exceeds all reason, He exceeds the greatest power, He exceeds the greatest need. When He does, He over does ("abundantly"), He out does. He goes beyond what is necessary. He provides beyond what is sufficient. He surpasses what is the natural limit. He overflows even the greatest need or lack. It's His nature. He doesn't do normal; He does abnormal. He doesn't do natural; He does supernatural. He doesn't do big; He does enormous. Here is a great example of His exceedingly abundantly trait. When the world's sin debt needed to be paid, and the amount of the debt being so great, and blood was the only method through which the debt could be atoned, (*"Without shedding of blood there is no remission."* - Hebrews 9:22), He didn't just send some blood that would be enough, No He sent the only blood type, type "JC positive," that would exceed the need and be abundantly able to atone for the world's sin debt, the blood of Jesus Christ. This is the same God that wants to use you in His kingdom. If what He does is always more than enough, then in choosing you He has determined that you have more than enough through Him to get the job done. And He is saying to you: Look "I Can", and with Me working in you "You Can".

A Technical Look

Through faith in His Son Jesus Christ and by the Holy Spirit born us again, God changed our failing nature, *"For all have sinned and fall short of the glory of God,"* (Romans 3:23) and bestowed upon us His overcoming victorious nature. *"For you are all sons of God through faith in Christ Jesus. For as many of you as were baptized into Christ have put on Christ."* (Galatians 3:26-27) He made us sons and daughters and provided us with a godly nature that we did not possess before. In biology, which is the study of living organisms and how they interact with their environment, the discipline focuses on every aspect of life in a living organism. Biologists tell us that the **genome** of an organism is the hereditary information of that ogranism that is encoded in

DNA. More specifically, human genome is comprised of two sets of 23 chromosomes or 46 chromosomes in all. Each parent contributes one set. We further understand through biology that **deoxyribonucleic acid,** or **DNA,** is a nucleic acid that contains the genetic instructions used in the development and functioning of all known living organisms and some viruses. The main role of DNA molecules is the long-term storage of information. DNA is often compared to a set of blueprints or a recipe, since it contains the instructions needed to construct other components of cells, such as proteins and other molecules. The DNA segments that carry this genetic information are called **genes**. Other DNA sequences have structural purposes, or are involved in regulating the use of this genetic information. They are called **Ribonucleic acid**, or **RNA.** The essential function of the RNA is to help the DNA. Stay with me, as I will reveal the relevance of this analogy in a moment. A gene is a unit of an organism's heredity and is a region of DNA that influences a particular characteristic in an organism. A gene is a sequence of DNA that contains genetic information and can influence the phenotype of an organism. A **phenotype** is any *observable characteristic* of an organism, such as its physiological properties, or behavior. I realize this is a lot of technical information, so I hope you are still with me.

Let's now draw some spiritual benefit from all of this technical information. Through Jesus' death, we were born again and became God's children. Note from the above information that of the chromosomes that are encoded on our DNA, half come from one parent and the other half from our other parent. Our natural earthly parents passed on to us their part, the part of mankind that includes sin (failure), however the other half of our chromosomes come from the unfailed, unflawed holy God who is our heavenly Father. We inhereted, through spiritual genetics, a new nature, unlike the human nature that is failure prone and has shortcomings. We received a new divine nature that empowers us to excel and accomplish what we could not before do and now exist being more than conquerors! *"As His divine power has given to us all things that pertain to life and godliness, through the knowledge of Him who called us by glory and virtue, by which have been given to us exceedingly great and percious promises, that through these you may be partakers of the divine nature."* (II Petter 1:3-4)

Again let us consider the above information that suggests that with DNA comes RNA. We know the primary function of RNA is to <u>help</u> DNA, or help to regulate the information encoded in the DNA. If DNA is our genetic instructions and determines our new nature, then we can relate the role of RNA to that of the Holy Spirit within us that helps us live our lives exhibiting this new nature. For Jesus said that He would be our "Helper," working to regulate the demonstration of our new God-given nature. *"But the Helper, the Holy Spirit, whom the Father will send in My name, He will teach you all things, and bring back to your rememberance all things that I said to you."* (St. John 14:26) The Holy Spirit helps us to fullfill our God-given abilities, and subsequently complete our God-given assignments. Whereas we were once failures by nature, we have now become winners by a new and more excellent nature.

DNA: God-given ability
RNA: God-given help = Holy Spirit
Phenotype: Observable Character traits

There is still more that we can glean from the above information. Let us again consider that a gene is a sequence of DNA that contains genetic information that influences the phenotype of an organism. And the **phenotype** is the *observable characteristic* of an organism, such as its behavior. We can now conclude that after being born again, we now have new genes that affect our observable characterics and behaviors. Therefore, if God is our Father, and His oberservable characteric is that He is able to get the job done, that means that part of our nature is being able to "do" as He "does."

Untapped Potential

A personally crafted statement I often like to make when teaching and instructing our congregation is: *"Unrealized potential is not potential at all."* This statement bears notice that if a person doesn't realize their potential, then to them it is not potential at all. A coach may see in his athletes a great deal of potential. He may commit himself to helping the athletes reach their full potential. The coach may work with the athletes daily to try to develop their skills and improve their performance. The coach may develop special workout regimens and assign restricted diets. All of the coach's efforts are designed to bring out of them the things the coach believes are still undiscovered. Unfortunately, with all of the coach's plans, and all of the coach's efforts, the athletes must accept and believe that they have the potential. No matter how much God sees in us, and knows what we can become in Him, and knows what we can do through Him, reaching that potential requires us to believe and accept that we have potential and abilities that have not been discovered. Similarly to the coach,

God will assign things for us to do that are designed to unleash those qualities that He knows are there. However, unlike the coach, who is limited to only being able to provide guidance to the athlete, God has the ability to not only guide but also supply through His Holy Spirit within us, the ability for us to accomplish things that without Him we would not be able to accomplish. God is the untapped potential that we have. He changes the whole game. He even changes the potential of the players in the game. When God is in the equation, it doesn't matter what we lack in ability or how many failures we may have had. Rather, when He wants to use us, He gives us a "potential transfer." That is, He transfers to us His potential where our potential falls short. Where we lack potential, He transfers His potential to that lacking area and causes us to function with "supernatural potential." With God's help, we are able to do things that are not "self-possible" but are "God-possible." We are no longer self-reliant, we become God-reliant. We can accomplish things that were not premeditated by us, but that were pre-obligated to us by God. The possibilities of what we can do are endless when we have God making up the difference.

God was calling Moses based partly upon Moses' potential and what He could see in him, however His calling of Moses was also based upon His potential in Moses.

"I will certainly be with you. And this shall be a sign to you that I have sent you: When you have brought the people out of Egypt, you shall serve me on this mountain."

(Genesis 3:12)

In the above scripture, God is trying to express to Moses that everything Moses does, God will be there assisting him. God was essentially saying to Moses: "I Can", so "You Can." Likewise, when He is calling you, He is basing that calling partially on your potential and what lies within you, but also the potential you posses in Him. As we often do, Moses underestimated the potential he possessed when being powered by God. As believers, we too often underestimate the power of God. We at times need to be reminded that if God is able to change our vile sinful nature and create in us a resemblance of Christ, it would seem to be no tall order for Him to use us.

God's Hands

"When I consider Your heavens, the work of Your fingers, The moon and the stars, Which You have ordained, What is man that You are mindful of him, And the son of man that You visit him?"

(Psalm 8:3-4)

"The heavens declare the glory of God; And the firmament shows His handiwork."

(Psalm 19:1)

With all that God has created and done without us, still He chooses to use us. If we would consider, as David does in these verses of Psalm 8 and Psalm 19, the great works of God's hands that He has done in the earth by having created the earth and all its splendor, we would begin to see how awesome His hands are and how magnificent the work is that has been created by those hands. If we would then also realize that it is those same hands that desire to work through us, we would be hard pressed not to get excited about being given something to do in the kingdom. Recognizing that it is our privilege to be a part of the magnificent works of God's hands is an essential part of developing and sustaining a lasting desire to be an instrument in the hands of our great God.

God's Tool Belt

Consider that a carpenter has many tools and that each tool serves a different purpose. The tools that he doesn't get much use out of he stores in his toolbox. It is not necessary to carry the less frequently used tools with him because he only uses them occasionally. However, a carpenter has a special place for the tools that he gets good use out of. He stores those in his "tool belt." He wears the tool belt around his waist for convenience, in order that he may to get to the tools quickly. The tools in the belt are used more frequently. The tools in the toolbox are tools nonetheless, however the tools in the belt are tools that he has worked with and is confident that those tools serve the purpose for which they were designed and crafted.

In the same way, Jesus is the *"Great Carpenter"* who has been assigned by His Father to lead and oversee the building of His kingdom, *"All things were made by Him; and without Him was not any thing made that was made."* (St. John 1:3 - KJV) God wants to use us as tools. Not only is God the Master Builder, but also He is the Master Craftsman, developing His tools through the work of the Holy Spirit. You and I are those tools. When we are not willing to allow God to use us in the way that He desires, He then places us in His toolbox that He may at some point again try to use us. On the other hand, when we are willing to be used by God and willing to be obedient to Him, He places us in His tool belt so that He may have greater access to us. It is a privilege to be in the tool belt of Master Builder, God Almighty.

Chapter Twelve

The Journey

After making the first step, then comes the journey that follows. That journey comprises the time in which you develop greater confidence in God's ability to accomplish even more through you. Although the first step is the hardest, as you continue to walk in obedience to God's calling, it will be necessary that you add to your faith continually; learning to trust God more and more each day.

> *"Finally, my brethren, be strong in the Lord and in the power of His might."*
>
> (Ephesians 6:10)

The word journey can be simplistically defined as moving from one place to another. Moving from where we are, and what we are doing, to another place. Doing something other than that which we have always done. Moving from how we trust God today, to how we will trust God tomorrow. Moving from feeling that our contribution will not make much difference, to knowing that doing it from the heart will matter greatly and that our contribution will be sufficient. Moving from not accepting

84

God's appeal to use us, to accepting and walking in step with whatever it is He desires of us. Moving from the pity party that I once hosted, to the celebration of the new things in God that I have done. Moving from not doing the undone, to doing the undone.

Trusting God is a journey, with many "trust stops." Each stop is built upon for the next. And moving on from each stop takes you further in the journey, and helps you to trust God more. Each "trust stop" is an exercise in trusting God, which produces experience, and experience produces hope, and hope in God will never make us ashamed. (Romans 5:3-4, KJV) Each exercise works to develop our trust muscle, which is our faith. However, faith doesn't automatically result in trust. Trust only happens through experience. Consider this practical application. You may have faith in your bank, which is probably why you chose that particular bank. But you don't necessarily trust your bank just because you have faith in its ability to safely handle your financial affairs. This is evidenced by the fact that each month you check your bank statement to make sure all of your accounts are correct and accurate. Having trust would be not needing the statements and not having to check the statements for accuracy.

With every hope-producing experience, your confidence in God's ability in you will grow. Just as trust happens the more you get to know someone and have positive encounters with their character, the same can be said of trusting in God. Trust in God will only happen as you continue to become better acquainted with Him and His ways each passing day of the journey.

Walking in obedience to what God has assigned you to do is a journey. It may begin, like Moses, with you not seeing it, or not being totally comfortable with it. Maybe you may have always had a calling in your heart but have just been reluctant to take the first step. No matter how the journey starts, it is still just that, the beginning. There will be high points and low points in the journey. Some days you will be excited and energized about what God is doing through you, and other days you may feel like somehow you are just not getting it done. The road may at times have hurdles, and even at times seem like an obstacle course, but seek assurance in knowing that God has equipped you and will equip you for whatever challenges you may face. He has the ability to lift you over hurdles, and to guide you successfully through any obstacle course. He has the supernatural ability to cause us to triumph in spite of adversity. *"Now thanks be to God who always leads us in triumph in Christ..."* (II Corinthians 2:14) Entrust that when your strength seems to fail you, and it seems that you no longer want to journey on, know that there is a remedy, *"I will go in the strength of the Lord God..."* (Psalm 71:16) These words of inspiration are important to be reminded of in the times of challenge and adversity. Knowing that you are serving Him, and therefore fulfilling the purpose He has for you, can go a long way in encouraging you in those times where it seems the wheels are falling off your wagon. In those times where you feel like giving up, stepping down from your post or resigning your position, remember to press forward relying on the strength of the Almighty God. Just imagine how Moses must have felt, after having submitted to the will of God for his life, and having walked in obedience to God. As he and the children of Israel are heading out of Egypt and he looks around and sees some 2 million Hebrew men, women, and children with their livestock and all of their possessions following him, and he recalls that God used him to help bring all of that about. I'm sure it must have been an amazing feeling, and only even more enhanced to know that it was all due to him having made the step beyond *"But What If I Fail"* to accepting that God wanted to use him and trusting God to use him. Moses would not have experienced the feeling of having been used by God in fulfilling His plan if he had chosen to not accept God's will for his life and remained where he was.

There is a confidence that can be experienced and exhibited by knowing and trusting that it is actually God's work (not our work) that He is accomplishing in us and through us. *"Being confident of this very thing, that He who has begun a good work in you will complete it until the day of Jesus Christ."* (Philippians 1:6) The work is His work, but He has chosen us as His agent to accomplish it. This confidence can help to silence the echoes of our fear of failure, fear of taking the first step, fear of the unknown, or even the realities of past failures. Because in the knowledge that God is working through us, we can find peace knowing that He has never failed at anything that He has wanted to accomplish, and that there is nothing that He has begun to do that has been left undone.

Writing this book has been a journey, one that began over three years ago. It hasn't taken three years because there was so much material to cover or research, or so many words to write, but it has taken three years because of my own struggle to realize and accept that when God is the thrust behind the effort, He is also the enabler. This book is also a part of my journey in ministry, a journey that began much like that of Moses, with me being reluctant and apprehensive about God's calling of me into the ministry. I struggled to see what God could already see in me, and was hesitant to accept the plan God had for my life because it didn't look like the plan I had. My journey has included my serving for several years as an associate minister, my having been used by God to plant a church, my now serving for several years as a Senior Pastor, and my now writing this book. The latter has quite possibly in some ways challenged and stretched me further than all the rest. For I have never considered myself much of a writer, and have been severely challenged just trying to sit and write, which is evident in my more than three-year struggle. However, it is also a testament of what God can do in us and through us when we are willing to allow Him to use us, for I have wrestled daily with the very question that titles this book **"But What If I Fail."** Asking questions that resembled those of Moses: "Do I really have anything worth saying in a book? Who will want to read it? Will anyone want to read it? Will it even get published?" Just to list a few. God has continually reaffirmed in me the message that is the common theme in this book. That when God desires to accomplish something through us, He is already aware of limitations, failures and fear we may have; yet He is still choosing us.

Through the writing of this book I have personally experienced the fear of failing, and have had to rely on knowing and believing that this is something God had assigned to my hands to do, and that I needed only to be obedient and allow Him to use me. I have learned even more so how to have trust in an assignment, by trusting in the Assigner. In order to find confidence in God's assigning of work to his followers, one must simply believe that if God is choosing them, then through him or her and with His divine help, it can be done.

Hopefully you have been inspired by this book to serve in an area that may be new to you, or to offer a gift, talent or skill to the Lord that you have not previously, or you have been encouraged to get back to the work of serving in God's kingdom. I would like to encourage you to move beyond the feeling of "But What If I Fail," and trust in the fact that you are not going it alone; rather, that God is the one who is using you, and He is the one who empowers you. My hope is that as you move forward after having completed this book that you too will: Trust God for something you have never before trusted Him, in a way you have never before trusted Him, to do something that you have never before done. And the journey moves on...How will you journey?
God Bless!

"Now may the God of peace who brought up our Lord Jesus from the dead, that great Shepherd of the sheep, through the blood of the everlasting covenant, make you complete in every good work to do His will, working in you what is well pleasing in His sight, through Jesus Christ, to whom be glory forever and ever. Amen."

(Hebrews 13:20-21)